T0078064

SPIRITUAL GARDENING

SPIRITUAL GARDENING

Cultivating the Path to Your Inner Journey

Caroline A. Baez, Esq.

To order additional copies of this book, contact:
Palibrio
1663 Liberty Drive
Suite 200
Bloomington, IN 47403
Toll Free from the U.S.A 877.407.5847
Toll Free from Mexico 01.800.288.2243
Toll Free from Spain 900.866.949
From other International locations +1.812.671.9757
Fax: 01.812.355.1576
orders@palibrio.com
756664

CONTENTS

"At the center of your Being you have the answer;
you know who you are
and you know what you want." ~ Lao Tzu

∞

Dedicated to my dear parents, my faithful
cabin mates on this beautiful journey,
and to my brother, whose soulful inner music awaits
to be released and bestowed upon the universe.

ACKNOWLEDGEMENTS

Luis Báez, my dear father: for your invaluable suggestions, your encouragement, and your unconditional support during this entire process. To all my lifetime teachers: for delivering lessons that contribute to my continuous spiritual growth. To all my spiritual teachers: for communicating with me through the language of silence across time and space, guiding me to the gateway of my peaceful, hidden treasure.

PREFACE

Today, as I read and organized my thoughts for this book's preface, I experienced a personal revelation, an intimate moment of illumination. I was concluding my readings on the method of surrender described by Dr. David Hawkins, a technique for letting go of all negative emotions which create obstacles in reaching our goals. Simultaneously, I thought of a recent TV interview where a panel of psychologists and experts discussed the inheritance of intergenerational psychological patterns. The experts proposed that we inherit psychological, emotional, and/or spiritual difficulties from our ancestors. They discussed that there is a whole intergenerational dynamic at play in our lives. This idea resonates with me as I have often reflected on the topic of physiological inheritance, on our DNA, and the memories recorded in our cells which are reproduced with traces of our ancestors. It is quite likely in this same manner that we inherit fragments of the psychology of our parents and their parents, having been raised under the personal framework of our parents' individualized life experiences and the tools which they, in turn, adopted to function within their own lives. Perhaps we also inherit fragments of our ancestors' spirits and perpetuate them across generations. We indeed inherit thought patterns not only from our parents and our families but also from our culture. There are also thought patterns associated with the social and political framework of the place in which we happen to be born and raised.

In that moment of personal reflection, I search within, keeping in mind the method of letting go of any negative emotions and the idea of intergenerational familial inheritance. I am aware that curiously because I have no children, any familial inheritance of negative patterns ends with me. Wonderful! This means that potentially, I will not be affecting/infecting any future generations with my emotional "garbage." Suddenly I ask myself, but how did it end up turning out this way? How did I end up making a series of personal decisions that resulted in an atypical lifestyle for a woman: remaining romantically unattached, maintaining a celibate lifestyle, not marrying or having children?

I reflect on the women in my family tree. The majority of them married and had children. The ones who never married, like my maternal and paternal grandmothers, were single mothers with a history of various romantic relationships and each of them with children from different fathers. This was highly unconventional behavior for women during my grandmothers' generation, and they were indeed judged harshly by their communities and society in general. Growing up, my parents too remember themselves being judged ruthlessly by children who inherited their sense of moral superiority and self-righteousness from their own parents.

Only a few years ago, I witnessed the aftereffects of the actions and decisions of our ancestors. Visiting my father's birthplace while on vacation, an elder recognizes my father. They chatted amiably reminiscing old times. Suddenly, the man mentions an ambiguously benign incident which, read between the lines, was evocative of my grandmother's personal love life.

After the encounter, my father explained that the individual's remarks were likely made in a malicious attempt to humiliate or hurt him, or perhaps to pigeonhole him into what he believed to be my father's rightful place by reminding him of his origin, as if to say, "I know who you are" in spite of any of my dad's personal advancements in life and notwithstanding the passage of time. You see, the man brought up an incident that alluded to a period in which my grandmother was rumored to have a lover. I had never known of the story until my father's revelation to me that day.

My dad then said to me, "Can you see now how karma follows us over time? Parents have no idea how much their mistakes end up hurting their children." We concluded that, although now deceased, my grandmother's karma still has its effects on my father, palpable effects that carry forward to a future generation years after my grandmother executed her actions, and those of us who are left behind must undoubtedly confront the aftermath of every unconscious action of the past. Whether consciously or unconsciously, we are inheritors of the pain, and we are responsible for either paying, transmuting, or transcending any negative karma inherited during our lifetimes.

I then proceed to ask myself, "If there is any, which negative karma have I inherited?" As I examine both my grandmothers' lives, I realize that I took the road less traveled. I avoided their mistakes. I am suddenly hit with a revelation. My grandmothers' mistakes ARE the reasons I am here! Had it not been for my grandmothers' "mistakes" or decisions, neither of my parents would have been born, nor would have the separate chain of events taken place that miraculously unfolded, individually disembarking my parents in this country, each of them far-removed from their own lands, ultimately joining two destinies which resulted in my own existence. Had it not been for those so called errors or decisions, I would have missed the opportunity of incarnating within this life experience, of existing, and of knowing my parents, my most beloved beings.

My eyes well up with tears upon this illuminating revelation—that I am a product of a series of complex, interconnected events across time and space, a miraculous manifestation of the mysterious and intricate unfolding of the Universe, and that there is a hidden perfection within imperfection and a secret order in chaos.

I realize that throughout my life, I have tried to be in control and to avoid making mistakes. Be it consciously or not, I tried to be "perfect" in the past, often making decisions cautiously, at times resulting in confusion and indecision, setting my course early on as a girl, perhaps in an attempt to avoid repeating my family's past. I did not select the unconventional path of the women in my family who were judged, but I also did not elect the traditional path chosen by the others, some of whom led unsatisfying, stifling lives as a result of choosing the "acceptable" path, the one designed by cultural and social mores for "good girls," yet, irrespective of their selected paths, many of them never actually felt completely self-fulfilled or happy.

In my desire to avoid taking a wrong turn, neither path was an attractive option for me as I was attempting to prevent future regrets, pain, suffering, and any negative inheritance resulting thereof for a next generation. My tears were tears of relief as I arrived at a newfound layer of personal understanding about my childhood, my adulthood, and my decisions throughout life.

At that moment, I understood that I needed to simply, let go, I needed to surrender the need for perfection and surrender all guilt ridden feelings for any supposed errors in my life. I can give myself permission to make decisions that are authentic to my personal judgment without the need to question whether they are correct or not because in fact, there are no correct or incorrect choices. Choices just ARE, and we cast our judgment on these decisions based on our own expanded or limited perceptions. I can give myself permission to embrace my perfect imperfections and receive chaos and its hidden order with open arms. I have the ability to escape any inherited patterns because these do not define me. I have the power to free myself from the trap of feeling shame as a result of the judgment of others because the opinion of others has neither the power to define us nor the power to limit us. Our true essence is wise, infinite, and unlimited. I can surrender myself to the unfolding of the Universe with complete trust because all is well and will continue to be well as long as I remain aligned to my true Self and the creative fountainhead of the Universe. I can choose to liberate myself from rigidity and the self-imposed expectations of my false "self", my ego, which is nothing more than a limited self-concept whose limitations are imposed by the mind. I have the right and the power to choose the path of freedom which is the inner path to my true essence—Pure or Infinite Consciousness.

Perhaps there are things that one is ashamed or embarrassed to reveal or admit to oneself, because of one's present or one's personal or inherited past, situations that one hide's because of fear of judgment, but one must be brave in order to remain authentic to oneself and strip the layers of suffering. So long as you do not muster the courage to penetrate deeply and reveal to yourself the patterns that create the roadblocks to your personal growth and spiritual progress, you cannot be entirely free.

Neither the negative patterns of your past nor the inherited patterns of your ancestors define you—you can escape them. We are our state of consciousness, a reflection of our intentions and of how we choose to process the world in which we live. Who we are is so much more expansive than the limited stories of our past and the limited stories of those from whom we descend. These stories do not predict that which proceeds from us. Problems and issues arise when you define and identify yourself by your personal and inherited past and with any external judgments about yourself and your life. The reason you identify with limitations and a false image of yourself is that you do not know your true origin and essence. Quite often, you fall into the trap of seeking external approval to validate your sense of self. When you value and internalize any external views about you, you become an unwitting accomplice in the unconscious act of pigeonholing and limiting yourself—you become the prison warden of your self-created prison.

While we may not be able to control how others perceive us, we definitely exert full control over our own perceptions of self and the world, and to that end, we are certainly responsible for digging deeply within to discover the wisdom, depth, and authentic power of our true Self. You are accountable for your state of consciousness, for your intentions, for your actions, for your choices, and for your internal, personal energy which radiates out and around you into the world. You are free when you align yourself with your true essence, beyond any self-imposed labels and beyond any labels derived from external sources. By cultivating your inner path to the blossoming garden of your own soul, you can manifest all your desires by creating, growing, and transcending to new and luminous horizons.

My desire is to share my revelations along my own inner journey to spiritual freedom—freedom from a self-imposed prison that we create as a result of depriving ourselves of deep, internal reflection, as a result of our innocence, as a result of not knowing how to turn the focus within to our Inner Master which resides within us all and which delivers revelations, guiding us through the language of silence and stillness, if we listen with our souls. Feeling grateful for this insight, for the opportunity to share my reflections on the path to true freedom, and with the intention that it serves the reader as a small guide, I wish you all, from this moment forward, a Happy Independence Day today and every day of your lives.

Love and Light,
Caroline A. Báez, Esq.
July 4, 2015

INTRODUCTION

In both a personal and professional context, I interact
with many people on a daily basis—clients, friends, and
family members—and I have observed in many the need
to establish a deep connection, the need to share and to
relieve themselves of their personal struggles. I have seen
an enormous amount of suffering. As an attorney in New
York, I offer legal and financial counseling to many, but
quite frequently, my services only provide solutions to a
layer of problems that often reflect symptoms of a deeper
level of suffering. I've consulted clients who begin to
reveal their personal pain about their relationships, their
families, their health, their general state of happiness, and
who sometimes even complain about what they consider
a harsh and bitter life. Many of these individuals seek
advice or at least a compassionate listener who can offer
comfort to relieve their sorrows.

This book is meant for all those whom, regardless of
enjoying the many pleasures life has to offer, reach the
conclusion that an integral piece is missing for a sense
of complete happiness, that something is not quite right,
individuals who feel that there is something more than
the daily grind and the ordinary routine of their lives

for a complete and self-fulfilled existence. Their instinct tells them that there is another dimension to life that eludes them, that they are in fact living a two-dimensional existence in a three-dimensional life.

These thoughts are actually quite natural because we ultimately conclude that we cannot obtain a permanent state of happiness from material things or from life's ephemeral pleasures. This is the first step leading to the exploration of other Elysian fields, of another Garden of Eden.

We lose nothing by exploring a new state of consciousness, a new and expansive vision of life; we instead have much to gain. Our reality (the world, the universe, life) is a mirror that reflects our view of life. When our vision is expansive and positive, our lives become a reflection of that same reality, and as such, that same mirror also reflects our perceived limitations, magnifying them in our lives like a high definition image.

WHERE TO BEGIN

What does the world need most? I say healing, not just physical, mental, and emotional, but also healing at the deepest level of our souls. Most people amble through life injured, in pain, suffering, complaining. These are all symptoms of illness. Sometimes we may be so accustomed to this state of existence that it often goes unnoticed and we accept it as a natural state of the human condition. Many accept suffering as an inevitable reality of life that cannot be escaped.

Unfortunately, our society conditions us to seek external remedies to heal our maladies. We are often searching for the miracle pill to lose weight or fight depression. We routinely observe the use and abuse of food, alcohol, or drugs to anesthetize emotional pain. We are indoctrinated with the idea of the "soulmate" to battle the emptiness of loneliness and conditioned with notions of the perfect house or the latest vehicle model to fulfill our idea of happiness, which is nothing more than an illusion of happiness that is sold to us, and which many of us have passively bought into and accepted as such. We end up purchasing and filling our lives with superfluous things that will never fill the inner void. "We buy things we do not need, with money we do not have, to impress people we do not like," as author Dave Ramsey's famous quote states. Nonetheless, none of this gets you any closer to the fullness of life and the happiness that you have always longed for and imagined attaining.

Much is spoken about achieving the "American Dream," or professional and economic success. Far less is spoken about attaining freedom from suffering and the key to happiness which resides within ourselves. One is hardly, if ever, taught how to turn one's focus within, and many neither understand what that means nor how to accomplish the daunting task.

The problem is that:

- We confuse who we are with the content of our minds.
- We confuse life with the content of our lives.
- We do not accept impermanence and change as something inevitable and natural.
- Suffering exists as a result of attachment and the fear of loss—fear of being deprived of people, situations, and things—all of which are impermanent.
- Nothing and no one can provide us with a true state of Happiness and Love.

An anecdote from my brother highlights this very point. My brother works as a law enforcement agent for the New York City penal system. One day, in the course of his daily duties, an inmate, upon observing the jail cell keys on my brother's belt, jokingly says to him, "Hey man, give me the key to get out of here!" My brother looks at him fixedly with a half-smile and with his typical sharp insight responds, "You've always had the key!" Surprised, the man detains himself in a sudden lightning flash-flood of thoughts provoked by the veracity of my brother's response. The surrounding inmates smile and nod their heads in agreement, each of them completely immersed in their own ruminations, transported far and away by the powerful currents of their own respective stories and inner dialogues. This anecdote always serves to me as a reminder that the simplest of truths eludes us perhaps because of its sheer simplicity.

Undoubtedly, whom we think we are determines the framework for the breadth of our views and our experience of life. As such, this work intends to provide the initial steps to reunite us with our Higher Self, liberate us from identifying with our ego, or "false self," and finally release us from old negative patterns and painful karmic inheritance. Through this freedom, we can experience the dynamic movement of our Infinite Being (Pure Consciousness) in this earthly, transient existence, leading us to a more awakened, happy, and expansive human experience. We initiate our return to this limitless state with an internal dialogue that responds to an intimate yet universal calling that whispers, beckoning from the depth of our soul, uniting us in an ancient yet timeless conversation that spans all eras.

To cultivate this path as a spiritual gardener means to sow seeds of well-being, to nourish and water positive intentions daily with love, compassion, and joy. By doing so, we will initiate intentions, thoughts, words, and actions that are attuned with whatever we wish to reap or manifest in our lives. It means to cultivate acceptance and responsibility with our daily choices as well as by evolving our awareness, all of which has holistic effects both individually and collectively as well as materially and spiritually. Through this inner journey, we rediscover the key that liberates us from suffering and opens the expansive gateway to the field of all possibilities.

I offer my reflections on the most influential teachers of my life with the intention that you find peace, love, abundance, and happiness. If it serves to confer a glimmer of light, if it contributes to discovering the Inner Master which resides within each of us, if it affords liberation from any negative programming, then this humble offering will have fulfilled its purpose.

1

PILGRIMAGE TO THE SELF BEYOND I: MY INNER JOURNEY

My personal journey, which I describe as a pilgrimage to my Self beyond "I" started like that of many others, it was prompted from suffering. I was under a lot of pressure in law school with an extremely demanding and exhausting student workload. I knew how to manage it, and I was succeeding because, ever since childhood, I had a very determined personality and a focused resolve to excel and succeed in whatever goal I set as my objective. On this occasion, as long as my mind was occupied on my academic goal, everything appeared to be perfectly sound. However, during my school breaks, when the scholastic pressure was not a factor, I felt that something was missing. It was a period in which I felt myself to be unhappy, lonely and with a desire to connect with people at a profound and sincere level. My expectations of happiness lay external to myself. In retrospect, I can see clearly that this was always the case, even as a little girl. I expected that, in the future, obtaining a professional degree, earning the coveted six-figure salary, living in the mansion of my dreams and having the man of my life by my side would furnish me with the happiness that I anticipated, as in all fairytales, of course.

During that same period, the attacks of September 11 took place; it shook New York, and my soul shuddered along with the city. I entered into what I consider an existential crisis. I had never felt the level of uncertainty and terror that I did that day in my entire life. Like many in my city and our nation, I believe to have lost a part of my innocence that day. We lost our innocence of feeling impenetrable. The hermetic cloak that protected us against the Axis of Evil was violently ripped apart. The illusory bubble in which we lived was forever ruptured.

I felt completely vulnerable and for the first time perceived the fragility of life like never before. I began to question my purpose and the purpose of life itself. Nothing made any sense. I felt depressed and had no desire to attend classes. What was the purpose of all my effort to excel with a high grade point average and obtain a professional degree if my life could very well be extinguished unexpectedly at any moment? What good did any of their efforts serve all those innocent, unsuspecting people who woke up, like any other Tuesday, only to meet their gruesome end? There were no guarantees in this life. We could end up planning our whole lives for nothing. This internal crisis was added to my general sense of insecurity and vulnerability.

The individuals with whom I associated and to whom I was attracted at the time revealed a series of unexplored thoughts and emotions within me. I was seeking security and approval from relationships, and I felt heart-broken and dejected by rejection. At the same time, I was surrounded by an atmosphere of constant tension and competition with whom I associated in law school, a defense mechanism of false power where my ego was highly activated. My ego was captivated by the ego of others. The egos of my admirers became fascinated with my ego. None of the relationships were based on our true essence. When our egos clashed, disappointment ensued; the ideal version of whom I had fallen in love would indeed shatter. Physical appearance, intellect, false humility, a sense of superiority to mask the inner feeling of inferiority—few of us, in fact, knew who we were. I now understand that we were relating from the level of our social masks. We were carrying the heavy emotional baggage of our past which reflected itself in our relationships.

Soon after experiencing a sentimental disappointment, I began a relationship which at first made me very happy and which I believed was finally filling the emotional void I felt inside. Nonetheless, over time, this relationship too began to reveal my flaws, just like an unforgiving close-up or the reflection of a mirror. I was blindly seeking completion through the relationship. It was a pattern of perceptions and thoughts that I was dragging along with me over time and which now emerged prominently as in high-relief. This was my turning point. When difficulties began to surface in my relationship, I was immediately confronted with my demons: attachment, insecurity, jealousy, distrust, the need for approval, guilt, anger, fear. Through this relationship I discovered that, I neither knew who I was nor what I really wanted and this scared me.

I became aware of the emotional emptiness that pervaded me and which no relationship could ever fill.

In an attempt to avoid making a mistake that I would later regret, I neither fully committed to the relationship to evolve it to a more serious level nor did I end it. My relationship remained in a state of limbo because of my indecision, and my boyfriend became frustrated because I did not clearly define my intentions. The situation was an impasse in my life. When I expressed my concern to my boyfriend, my need to find myself because I did not know who I was and was uncertain of where I was going, he reassured me that all I really needed was to finally commit and be with him, and this only heightened my confusion.

Undoubtedly, I was seeking security, love, and happiness outside of myself when in fact everything I needed was already within me. No matter how much he would have liked, this man could never give me what I actually needed, that which I needed to rediscover for myself on a personal journey, on a solitary pilgrimage to the inner depth of my Self. I would have never understood this had it not been for my naïve desire to find myself, to find self-fulfillment through him.

For the first time, I realized that it was possible to be with someone yet feel alone. Eventually, I began to feel emptiness in his embrace; I felt him distant and disconnected as if he were merely attempting to mirror my apparent need for a deep connection. Sometimes I felt that he looked at me but did not truly see me. I felt invisible and alone, but I do not blame him for this. The truth is that I was naively imposing on him a responsibility that was not actually his, the responsibility to complete me—an impossible task to fulfill. I had certain expectations of him, which I did not disclose, and yet which I expected him to meet, as if he were a magical diviner of my emotional needs, the one held accountable for rescuing me from my internal dragons and fulfilling the implicit promise of a "happy ever after" to my fairytale.

I am now aware that, within my former state of consciousness, I was unable to offer anything of real value to a relationship. I did not know it at the time, but I was unconsciously playing roles—loveable me, sexy me, funny me, smart me, witty me, playful me, flirty, naughty me. As in past interrelations with any romantic potential, I doubted myself in his presence, feeling as though I were trying to measure up to his undisclosed, ideal-soul-mate litmus test. How long could this last? The charade was exhausting! I felt as if I were posing throughout the relationship in a series of still lifes, their romantic beauty frozen in time, flat and two-dimensional, with no possibility for movement or expansion.

Ultimately, I alone was responsible for imposing this burden on myself, fearing that I would not measure up to my?, his?, ideal version of, "me." I alone was responsible for objectifying myself. At the time I thought to myself that if being in a relationship was supposed to make me happy, and if my experience exemplified what relationships were like, then the experience was highly overrated and fell short of all my expectations. The experience felt shallow and unsatisfying. I knew that this was not happiness. In retrospect, I understand that my emotions, perceptions, and expectations were rooted in darkness and the unconsciousness of my ego or false self.

Looking back, I now realize that I was never actually present in the relationship and without presence there is no opportunity to "see" deeply what cannot be seen with the eyes of mere mortals. Ultimately, one's desire is to "see" oneself reflected in the other, to "see" and spiritually "feel" through a truly deep and soulful connection. I began to feel that I was being dragged by the current of our romance, waiting for calmer, deeper, and more transparent waters. Sometimes I didn't feel like myself in his presence. I felt uncomfortable in my own skin, uneasy and out of place, as if I needed to fulfill his, as of yet, undisclosed standards and expectations—quite likely a product of my own projection, but, who was I really? This had been undiscovered territory until this point. I had yet to navigate the deep, uncharted waters of my soul, of Being itself. After the relationship ended, a new phase began for me, one of self-discovery. Thus began my inner pilgrimage to my Self beyond "I." It is here that I start to cultivate the spiritual path to my inner journey. It is here that I begin to heal and to see with more clarity.

It would be quite easy to vilify and blame the actions and omissions of those with whom I interacted during that phase of my life. It would also be easy to bemoan and blame myself without assuming any responsibility for my personal role in those events—without taking responsibility to grow and expand as a result of those past experiences. The truth of the matter is that perhaps none of the parties involved behaved ideally, but we couldn't expect any of the participants to behave any differently than what our respective states of consciousness allowed at the time. I now understand that we were operating from our egos, each one seeking to find in the other that which they desired or thought they needed at the time. The important thing is that each relationship, whether romantic or not, is a mirror that reflects exactly where we need to heal, learn, transform, expand, and transcend. In fact, it is our reactions to the behavior of others that furnish us with the most substantive life lessons. Our reactions and emotions give us the opportunity to delve deeply within and expand to a state of consciousness of wholeness and self-fulfillment.

It is now evident to me that every brief encounter with each person in this lifetime is necessary for our individual journeys to self-discovery, growth, and true Love. No experience is ever lost or wasted on us. Nothing is ever truly gained or deprived. Each layer of pain, suffering, laughter, and joy contributes to our evolution and the expansion of our state of consciousness or awareness. Every decision, every action and encounter leave their trace and guide us along the way to either our destruction or our salvation, to the prison of our own making or to our freedom. Each of us has our own share of responsibility in our mutual self-creations, like co-responsible accomplices along with every other intersecting, seemingly random individual and apparently fortuitous circumstance that maneuvers itself in and out of our daily lives.

I realize that I have been delivering, giving birth to myself, through each experience. I understand that each chapter in my life has been necessary, of which I have no regrets. There are no errors in life. Each episode has served as a portal to my Self, of which I am grateful. Every life experience, whether integral or not, forms part of a design element in the intricate tapestry of our lives where the independent significance of each experience is imperceptible as such, when viewed from a distant vantage point, yet, upon closer examination, one sees each element woven subtly throughout the whole, contributing an additional dimension of texture and richness that adds to the tapestry's unique pattern and beauty.

We are each on our own individual journeys and therefore all "alone" in that regard, like lone journeymen processing the world through our eyes and minds. We alone are responsible for this voyage and where it takes us. Ultimately, we are all seekers, seeking the same things—the way back home, the way back to wholeness. We lose our way by searching in the wrong direction, by seeking outside of ourselves for a sense of completeness through other people and through material things or both. As a society, we are conditioned towards object-referral rather than self-referral.

We are programmed as a society to seek love and happiness outside ourselves, but one can only seek that which one believes to lack. We are rarely taught that love and happiness already reside within us, we merely need to re-discover it by turning our focus inwardly. I love a quote by Chinese Buddhist Master Tai Xu, "As long as the tree is behind you, you can only see its shadow. If you want to touch reality, you have to turn around." We must turn around to ourselves, to the place where we've always held the key to our freedom and an awakened, expansive state of consciousness. You enter this state of being, this intimate space, from wherever you happen to be. You do not need to go anywhere special or do anything grandiose to witness this inner spaciousness. You only need to be present and still. Here begins the simple yet often elusive internal pilgrimage to the depth of Being that is one's Higher Self, or as I call it, the Self beyond "I."

2

SUFFERING:
THE PATH TO FREEDOM

"The wound is the place where the
Light enters you." ~ Rumi

RECOGNIZING SUFFERING

The first step on the path to freedom involves recognizing and facing our suffering. When I speak of suffering, I not only refer to suffering as a result of a major crisis or traumatic life events but also the type of inner pain that often lays quietly hidden inside and is not always apparent to others. There are different levels of suffering, some more subtle and transient than others, and perhaps on many occasions we have all faced moments of inner pain in our lives. Some people may suffer because of a physical condition, illness, death of a loved one, or a difficult financial situation. Some may suffer due to loneliness while others may suffer as a result of toxic relationships. Parents often suffer for their children and many sons and daughters suffer for their parents. Sometimes suffering results from memories that seem to trap us in an endless cycle of pain that appears to scar us for a lifetime. Many times suffering is tied to past resentments or remorse. Other times we may suffer anxiety about our uncertainty over the future. We suffer whenever we feel shame, disappointment, boredom, sadness, fear, jealousy, envy, anger, hatred, guilt. We may surely experience this entire emotional spectrum in the span of a whole lifetime, or perhaps even experience a lifetime's worth of emotions in the span of a single day.

We may ask ourselves, is it necessary to accept these emotions as an integral part of the human condition? Must we resign ourselves to a life burdened by suffering as an intrinsic part of our existence, like a life-term prison sentence? The answer is a categorical, no! There is a way to free ourselves from this self-created prison, and the key resides within ourselves. The first step is, to be honest with oneself, step out of denial when we experience any form of suffering, acknowledge the pain, admit that we wish to improve our condition and that we deserve to feel whole and therefore, be willing to discover the key to freedom and true Happiness. It requires acceptance and courage on our part, in facing the condition or conditions causing our suffering, and responsibility for undertaking the path to transformation. As Rumi's quote states at the beginning of this chapter, our wounds provide the proper gateway for the Light to enter and guide us towards healing and the path to freedom. You start your path as of now, from wherever you happen to be no matter what your current life situation is. You start cultivating the path to your inner journey to liberate yourself from suffering through tenderness and patience. Irrespective of your present circumstances, wherever you find yourself at this moment, your starting point for this inner journey is here and now.

WHY DO WE SUFFER?

The main reason we suffer is that we do not know who we are. We believe ourselves to be that which we are not: our bodies, our thoughts, our gender, our professional title, our social-economic status, our roles as employees, parents, sons and daughters, spouses, etc. We identify with our names, our race, our nationality, our culture, our political parties, our material acquisitions or our mere lack of them. However, all of these things and labels are transient and do not encompass our true essence. By defining ourselves in terms of these limited concepts, we become prisoners of our own definitions or of the definitions and labels imposed on us, and which we accept, from the outside world. As a result, our reality and life experience are limited to the extent of our own self-imposed margins drawn by a narrow vision of ourselves.

All of these material things and labels with which we identify ourselves are ego based, and the ego is nothing more than a false and limited sense of self. We all have an ego, and the ego's existence depends on defining itself in terms of its thoughts and the acquisition of material things in order to expand or broaden its identity or self-concept. We begin from the premise that we are incomplete and therefore the more things and labels we acquire, the more "ourselves" we feel. However, this is an erroneous premise. We are not our egos, and we are not incomplete.

We confuse who we are with the content of our minds, but the content of our minds, the knowledge, and thoughts we store, are simply tools used to navigate the physical world that we perceive with our senses. We confuse our lives with the content and conditions of our lives, but the content and situations of our lives are transitory and constantly changing. As such, they can never provide us with a firm and permanent identity. Our ego drives us to look outside ourselves for answers to our troubles and anxieties, to search for people and things to feel whole, to alleviate our suffering and fill the inner emotional void.

However, searching outside of ourselves, in the material world, we find things, fleeting pleasures and people who often provide only temporary relief and happiness. As soon as the transient effect subsides, a new cure must be sought to relieve the suffering and once more attempt to fill the emptiness. Undoubtedly, the cycle repeats itself because the cure is merely provisional serving only as a palliative treatment to alleviate and temporarily eliminate symptoms of a deeper malaise or disease. To truly heal, one must cure the disease from the root rather than treat the symptoms. Do not fear your suffering; it is the portal to your transformation, your opportunity to transcend old patterns and unfruitful perceptions—it is the gateway to your rebirth into a new life.

The next step required to walk out of this endless cycle is to recognize and explore the reality that lies beyond the physical world and beyond the ego. We must see the Light and walk in its direction to merge with it as one.

3

TURNING YOUR
FOCUS WITHIN

"I am not this hair, I am not this skin, I
am the soul that lives within…" ~ Rumi

Who are you? Initiating from this point of origin,
we subscribe to a paradigm which either limits and
imprisons us or instead contributes to our expansion
and freedom. This basic yet universal question unites
us in an endless conversation that spans across time. Do
you consider yourself a conglomerate of nerves, bones,
muscular and brain synapses, a biological evolution of
complex thoughts, an exclusively carnal being? Do you
consider yourself an expansive, spiritual being who is
part of an intelligent, interconnected evolutionary web of
Divine expression? Do you consider yourself a physical
being who has occasional spiritual experiences or a
spiritual being who is living a temporary, impermanent
earthly experience? How you respond to these questions
characterizes the tone of your world, the meaning,

---

and purpose of your existence and determines your experience of life. If you decide that you are your ego, your body, or your mind, your personal reality will be limited by a human experience that only encompasses the physical world as experienced through your senses. This is not to say that this reality is wrong or inferior, but it does only reach a limited stratum of a greater, more expansive reality. If you recognize yourself as a divine being living a temporary human existence, your experience will broaden to a human experience that includes the world beyond physical reality, moving you towards a more expansive spiritual reality that allows you access to the abundance of the Universe and freedom from suffering.

Nonetheless, the good news is that we do not have to choose between a material and spiritual world. In this earthly, human manifestation that we are living, we are, in fact, experiencing a miraculous dimension of Divine expression. The point is to recognize that we can live with an awakened awareness, with a consciousness of dynamic Divinity that is made manifest by its movement and circulation through us by means of our human experience—what I call a state of conscious humanity. At this state, we are able to experience the symbiotic relationship between our earthly and spiritual dimensions. It is possible to live a holistic experience, nourishing body, mind, and spirit through conscious (mindful) consumption at both our spiritual and material levels, which we will explore later on. As such, we may thoroughly enjoy the wholeness of our spiritual-material duality which we have been miraculously allowed to experience within this small parenthesis in eternity we call life.

EGO: THE FALSE SELF

The ego is our sense of identity in the physical world that we experience with our senses. The ego is comprised of two elements: the function of desiring and its storehouse of possessions. We may compare the ego to a capricious child whose insatiable function is to desire everything it sees at shopping centers. Its function is to desire and demand whatever captivates its attention and imagination. When the child obtains the sought after toy, a period of satisfaction and happiness ensues, but this is a fleeting emotion because soon enough the toy loses its initial brilliance and charm and the child focuses his attention on whatever new toy catches his eye. It does not matter how many toys this fickle child has accumulated over time. When he takes inventory of his vast storehouse of toys, all of them bore him. The child always needs and desires some other toy to make him happy. Similar to a capricious child, the ego is comprised of the fundamental and insatiable function of perpetually desiring and the warehouse of labels, objects, and symbols that it accumulates in an attempt to build-up its identity and broaden its sense of self. The warehouse refers to the things and symbols themselves that contribute to the ego's sense of self or identity. For example, with whatever "I" identifies, or whatever is "mine" serves as an "added-value" enhancement to the ego.

The ego is a formation of the mind whose existence is grounded on perceptions and thought patterns about the past and the future. The ego operates in the physical world in what can be described as the horizontal dimension that we experience as the physical reality of space-time. The ego's existence depends on the concept of time because the ego defines and expands or limits its sense of self by both its past or history or by whatever it anticipates or desires in the future. The ego is never satisfied with the current state of affairs or with the conditions of the present moment—it never feels satisfied or "enough" in and of itself and never feels that it possesses enough stuff. The ego is never satisfied until it obtains its intended goal or desire, but once reached, the objective loses its charm, and the inner void once again seeks something new to accomplish or possess. The ego seeks temporary cures for the disease of chronic dissatisfaction.

Every spiritual path, every road to liberation, requires taming or eliminating the ego. When we eliminate the ego, we penetrate the true nature of our essence, of our Higher Self which is Divine Wisdom, a spark of Divine Oneness. We penetrate into what, until this point, remained concealed as a result of negative programming adopted throughout the history of humanity, namely: competition, envy, anger, pride, guilt and mistrust. It is by taming our ego and turning our focus within that we discover our true nature, where we operate from the higher states of consciousness of Love, Peace, Happiness, and where cooperation, harmony, kindness, compassion, trust in oneself and the Universe abides.

I AM: THE HIGHER SELF

"Become nothing, and he will turn
you into everything" ~ Rumi

In his quote, the Persian poet and Sufi master Rumi reveals to us that by discarding what we are not, we arrive at what we truly are. Beyond our physical world and beyond the labels and roles with which we identify, we are, in essence, the space that allows the content of our thoughts. Thoughts are like floating clouds which disappear into the expansive background of the blue sky. In the same way, our Higher Self is like the infinite blue vastness above us, a spaciousness that knows no bounds or limits. In our true essence, we are the gap between each thought, the space that abides silently between each breath. This space is pure consciousness—consciousness that transcends thought and ego—it is a higher state of awareness which observes silently, nonjudgmentally and with detachment. This is the I AM state of pure, infinite, awakened consciousness, the empty space that contains all the universal information and infinite wisdom of Divine Intelligence.

This higher state is our true essence. This deeper ground of awareness is our genuine nature prior to having been conditioned and adulterated by negative patterns and by the personal human experience we so happen to inhabit and live. At the level of Pure, Infinite Consciousness, our essence is a state of oneness that reconnects with the well-spring of our Being, a source which some call Universal Intelligence, Field of Oneness, Divine Intelligence, Undifferentiated Consciousness, Tao, or God, among others. When we reconnect with this infinite state of consciousness, we simply ARE at the purest level; we realize that we are One with Divine Creation and are therefore complete. When we awaken to this state of higher awareness, we recognize that we are part of a perfect universal symphony and that we are essentially divine beings temporarily manifested in human form in this material world. Awakened to this new state of enlightened awareness, we live in the physical world but with an expansive consciousness that also includes an absolute reality that exists beyond what we physically perceive through our senses, allowing us access to unlimited abundance and true freedom.

In order to access or reconnect with our essence—our Higher Self—we must turn our outer focus inwardly; we must deviate our attention from the external world of our sense perceptions, of the material reality we perceive, and into our inner space. What does it mean to turn our focus inwardly and how does one accomplish this seemingly abstract and daunting endeavor? First and foremost, the task requires us to stop seeking external solutions for our suffering and for remedies that simply temporarily mask any inner emotional emptiness or pain. This means that we must stop identifying with factors external to ourselves, it means not depending on the approval of others, or on material things or labels in order to validate our lives or validate our sense of self. When we turn our life's focus from the external world to the wealth of our inner world, our Higher Self becomes our inner compass, guiding our intentions, our decisions, and our life's purpose.

SILENCE AND STILLNESS

Our inner space is where we access our true state of Being or Higher Self. Our Higher Self is the inner master that resides within each of us, in the divine sanctuary of our internal space, our infinite source of wealth and wisdom. We can access this inner space through silence and stillness.

When we silence the turbulence of our minds and calm our bodies and our breath, we reconnect with our true essence.

Divine wisdom speaks to us through silence and stillness unveiling depth of Being, an eternal Self, a Higher Self that has always been and will continue being, beyond the fleeting world of forms. It reveals to us our oneness with life itself and with all that is.

"Silence is the language of God…all
else is a poor translation" ~ Rumi

"Be still and know that I am
God" ~ Bible, Psalms 46.10

Sufi poet Rumi and the book of Psalms point to the same truth. Silence and stillness are the portals to true, unlimited Love, Happiness, Peace, and Freedom. When we access our inner space and rediscover our true self, we reconnect with our natural state of wholeness. In that inner space, we remember that which we have forgotten as we travel through this transient world wearing the illusory mask of our egos. We rediscover our intrinsic value and our authentic power. In this inner space, it becomes evident to us that our external world cannot offer true love, validation or self-fulfillment because the physical world perceived by our senses is impermanent and its pleasures are ephemeral. Silence and stillness are the keys to an unrivaled treasure that resides within us all and which is always accessible NOW.

Why do we escape silence and stillness when it happens to be the gateway to our true Self? Our ego, or false self, fears quiet and stillness because, in this space of inner presence, the mind comes face to face with its unconsciousness, it becomes aware of its unease where the level of turbulence, pain, and dysfunction is magnified. You will likely observe that when your mind enters into silence, the mind initially fires into a whirlwind of thoughts. You will notice that the mind frequently presents resistance when your body seeks stillness, instead trying to say or do anything to fill the apparent sense of emptiness. For example, some people turn on their TV's or stereos as soon as they wake up in the morning. Some constantly check their smart phones for messages and social media updates. If they are waiting in line at the bank or at the doctor's office, they find the need to establish a conversation to fill the time. Some people turn up their car stereo to its maximum volume in order to envelop themselves fully in the music. On their return home and prior to bedtime, many turn on their TV once more in order to fall asleep. These are all examples of escapism, of resistance to the space of quiet stillness where we encounter the field of Pure Consciousness (Infinite Consciousness), the dwelling place of our true essence or Higher Self.

Ego resists crossing the gateway to your true essence because it fears its destruction. It is in this still space that you reconnect with your Higher Self and your authentic power where ego holds no actual power or strength. In this space, problems begin to dissipate because, in that state of higher awareness, you are whole and nothing is lacking. Ego suffers from spiritual myopia and, as such, it maintains its focus on magnifying the external world, attempting to broaden its sense of self by distracting you away from yourself, away from your true Self. As long as you remain wholly focused on and identified with the external world that you perceive through your senses, you will remain in the dark prison of ego's own making.

The following lists describe the characteristics and differences between a human experience that is aligned with

Pure Consciousness and characteristic of the Higher Self (Infinite Consciousness) and a human experience aligned with ego or the false self.

PURE CONSCIOUSNESS	EGO
Higher Self	False Self
Identity: Divine Essence	Identity: Labels and Roles
Deeper Needs	Superficial Needs
Focus: Present	Focus: Past and Future
Silence and Stillness	Escapism in the Physical World
Whole/ Self-Actualized	Incomplete/ Missing Parts
Independent	Dependent on External Factors
Freedom	Mind Created Prison
Absolute Truth	Relative Truth
Eternal and Infinite	Impermanence, Limitation
Field of All Possibilities	World of Duality
Universal Love, Compassion	Exclusive Love, Egotism
Fulfillment through Oneness	Individualized Fulfillment
Integrity/Equality	Separation/Differences
Happiness and Spiritual Growth	Fleeting Pleasures
Dharma	Karma
Life with Purpose	Human Unconsciousness
Detachment	Attachment
Spiritualism	Materialism
Faith, Trust	Distrust, Skepticism
Surrender	Resistance

Individuals who align with ego and who attach themselves mainly to the physical world, generally self-define themselves in terms of their roles and other external labels. The ego is strengthened by any possessions and positions held in society as well as by devaluing others, oftentimes measuring individuals by personally held judgments and perceptions that are based on a limited scale of values. For example, they measure a person's worth in terms of their manner of dress, the car they drive, the neighborhood in which they live, the prestige of the university from which they graduated, their type of employment and salary level, among other factors. Certainly, you may have likely observed people around you or in the media who derive their sense of importance and superiority from their social or economic position, from their fame or fortune, from a professional title, because they own numerous properties, because they own or lead a popular music group, because they are celebrities, because they are CEO's of a large corporation, because they are president of a company or perhaps the president of a nation, to name a few. Oftentimes, their attachment to these labels as a form of identity, to ego, is so pronounced that their final attempt is to leave their legacy behind in order to perpetuate themselves in the physical world long after they have moved past their physical existence. What happens when these individuals lose their positions, their possessions, money or fame? Their sense of identity disintegrates, their sense of self becomes lessened, and their concept of self shrinks. Under these new circumstances, it is common for the ego to adopt a new identity, a victim identity, perhaps an inferiority complex, often presenting resistance in the face of any subsequent unfolding of undesirable events. There may be feelings of anger and sometimes depression.

An individual who at one time demonstrated an exalted sense of superiority comes to mind. He was a quite successful real estate broker. He dressed well, prided himself in his two luxury cars of the latest model, and because of his position and elevated standards, he made it quite clear that he expected the best and highest level of personalized service as a client. In 2007, the real estate and financial institution debacle takes place in the U.S., resulting in an avalanche of repossessions, home foreclosures, the dramatic devaluation of properties, the plummeting of the stock market, the economic recession and financial crisis, the rise of personal and business bankruptcies, and with all this, the inevitable decline of the real estate market. This individual became unrecognizable. He gained weight, and his self-esteem dropped, the energy of his overbearing personality was replaced by shame, despondency, and depression. His two luxury cars were repossessed, and he was in danger of losing his home. His real estate business had crumbled, and his marriage was in crisis. This man was suffering.

As illustrated by this example, so long as we live entrenched in ego, identifying with our possessions and with false notions of self, we will remain rooted in an illusory sense of identity and false power. We must instead demolish our false foundations and dismantle the altars we have built to honor the false images of ourselves. We must end our blind idolatry of ego, and our worship of the shadows that make up the material world, the external world of forms. We must destroy old patterns in order to reconstruct and transform our experience of life. Only by dissolving our ego will our true essence emerge, the state of Pure Consciousness which is the heart of our authentic power and wisdom. Living from this newfound state of your Higher Self, you will partake in true confidence regardless of the circumstances of your life, the impermanence of material things and transitory pleasures.

Individuals who align themselves with the true essence of Pure Consciousness are easy to distinguish because their lives reflect their essence. These individuals are positive and optimistic, and as such, life seems to smile at them. Their fruitful results are self-evident. They are generally healthy—and should they suffer from some ailment, they accept it without either defining or victimizing themselves in terms of the disease—and they feel whole and self-fulfilled without it being necessary for their goals or accomplishments to fit the typical mold of success that society impresses upon us. These individuals exhibit an authentic confidence because their Higher Self is their True North on the inner compass that guides their life's journey, and as such, they have no need for external approval of their lives or their decisions. They have no life complaints even when difficult situations arise because they trust that there is a solution for everything, they remain calm in the face of life's occasional storms. These individuals are open and receptive to others. They are compassionate and loving with everyone and rarely experience problems with their interpersonal relationships. In their professional or work relationships, they enjoy what they do, are cooperative, and seek creative and beneficial solutions where others find none. Their words and actions are grounded in the positive energies of highest frequencies. As such, the lives of these individuals are a harmonious reflection of the same energy they radiate out into the world. It is a state of peace and harmony that cannot be improvised. You can reach this state of light and advancement, it is your inherent right as a child of Divine Creation, and it is the key to true freedom where you will break free from the prison of darkness to create your own paradise here on earth.

You can begin to access the state of Pure, Infinite Consciousness in the inner space where your Higher Self dwells by practicing silence and stillness. Within that inner space, you will encounter and submerge yourself in that which you truly are. This is your access point to begin cultivating your inner garden so that it may bloom into the maximum expression of your soul, endowing you with a limitless bounty of fruitful rewards.

EXERCISE

"Calm the waters of your mind, and
the Universe and the stars will be
reflected in your soul." ~ Rumi

SILENCE AND COMMUNION WITH NATURE

One helpful exercise is taking a little time out of each day, either upon rising, after work or before bedtime, to quiet your mind and your breathing for 5 to 10 minutes. Over time, you may increase the duration of silence to 30 minutes or ideally for longer. This exercise will help you to penetrate the inner space where your true essence will reveal itself to you beyond the endless downpour of thoughts that typically inundate your mind. Whenever thoughts arise and overwhelm your mind, simply observe them without judgment and without holding on to any of them. Let the thoughts float by like clouds in the sky.

Experiencing silence and stillness in nature can also provide an exceptional experience that has personally proven very valuable to me. The time spent communing with nature has presented me with the most blissful moments of silence and stillness. The natural sounds of the ocean's tide, the breeze, birds signing, or a majestic sunset before dusk all help to quiet the mind and calm our breathing. In such moments of inner peace and calm, you rediscover your Higher Self and are nourished by a deep replenishing energy in the process. It is in moments such as these where it becomes revealed that you are indeed a part of something much greater and perfect, the Divine Symphony of the Universe.

MEDITATION: I AM

Sit or lie down comfortably with your palms facing up. Close your eyes and breathe naturally, relaxing your body. After calming your body and your breathing for 1-2 minutes, silently introduce to your mind the idea, "Who am I?" Different thoughts will come to mind, perhaps your name, your gender, your role as parent or spouse, your nationality, or professional title, amongst others. Let all these labels and identifications pass by without judging or attaching yourself to any of them, letting them flow and dissipate slowly without forcing them for 2-3 minutes. Then silently introduce the idea, "I Am," for approximately 5-10 minutes without adding any labels or descriptors after the phrase. Silently observe what happens each time you introduce the phrase, concentrate on your breathing. Observe the silence and the gap that follows between each thought as each one subsides and before another arises. Observe the space between each inhalation and exhalation within silence and stillness. Each time a new thought arises, let it float by like a cloud. Whenever you become distracted, reintroduce the phrase, "I Am," and observe your mind without judging or censoring it. After 20 minutes, open your eyes gently, closing your meditation. Practice this meditation daily for 10-20 minutes, or for any amount of time you are otherwise able to manage, to penetrate deep into your inner space.

With longer and more consistent practice, you will observe that the gap between each thought will stretch. The intention is for you to become one with the silent space. In that gap, you will become aware of the serene background that allows the content of your thoughts to take shape in your mind. You will realize that you are neither your thoughts nor the labels with which you have long identified along your life's journey, but rather the observer (awakened consciousness) behind those thoughts. This serene backdrop is the field of Oneness, the depth of your Pure and Infinite Consciousness—your Higher Self.

4

THE MAGNITUDE
OF INTENTION

Your intention is design in embryo,
engendering everything you create.

Every word, every action, every decision begins with
an intention. Thoughts, words and actions are all energy
and, whether consciously or not, they convey the same
energy as our intentions. Understanding the power of
intention is indispensable for us to behold the abundance
of the Universe in our lives. The Universe uncovers the
true energy of our intentions even when these happen
to be unconsciously held. Therefore, we should always
exercise mindful awareness of the underlying intentions
of our desires. Every intention that you convey into the
Universe attracts an identical energy to yourself because it
joins an energy field that shares the same affinity in order
to create your will and materialize it in the physical world.

Our intentions are comprised of our will and what we
value most. Our intentions are a reflection of our sate of

consciousness, which in turn is based on our perceptions of self, of the world and our conception of reality. Our intentions carry the energy of our will and of our desire to obtain everything we want out of life. If, for example, your aspiration is to become a great entrepreneur, or a great athlete, the energy of your intention is what propels all of your thoughts and actions, invading every corner of your consciousness with the planning and execution of your goal. We must, therefore, be clear with our intentions to obtain fruitful results. Each time we make a decision, we radiate the most clandestine energies concealed in our hearts. With each decision we emit our energy, setting it in motion and out into the world, contributing to the unfolding of an infinite series of developments in the intricate web that connects us all. This implies a profound responsibility, not only at the personal level but the collective level as well—of our families, our society, our nation and our world.

We are consistently making decisions daily, interacting with people, and actively participating and creating in our lives. We are all simultaneously directing our energy externally to others, through decisions that are impelled by our intentions. The individuals with whom we interact in our interpersonal relationships, in our employments, in our casual encounters, all absorb our energy and process it according to their own states of consciousness and project it forward, by that means, continuing the perpetual movement of energy, each one of us sharing our mutual co-responsibility in the co-creation of the world in which we live.

Our intentions can either be rooted in ego or in our Higher Self. Intentions can be charged with either positive or negative energy. For example, an intention based on hatred, anger or envy propels thoughts and decisions that result in effects that are tantamount to the energy of the originating intention. In contrast, an intention based on compassion, unconditional love, or peace, sets in motion the flow of positive energy that is in harmony with the Divine fountain spring of creation and as such, the effects will have the same affinity, as a result of the shared frequency. We can compare our intentions with seeds which we water and nurture with our own energy. These form strong roots that grow into lush, bushy trees, producing bountiful fruits for our harvest. You cannot expect a harvest of sweet oranges if you plant and cultivate seeds of sour lemons.

As long as our intentions remain rooted in supplying the needs of our ego, we will be operating at a frequency that will manifest effects of comparable energy, of a limited consciousness where nothing satisfies us completely and where the effects of our actions are generally fruitless. The reason for this is that intentions that originate from ego proceed from an unconscious human existence where we ignore our true essence and as such, they derive from a state of scarcity or poverty consciousness. Intentions proceed from this limited state when we are unaware of the natural flow of the universe and the universal spiritual principles. The spiritual principles of the universe are the operating system or laws of the cosmos, the principles that move creation. These are principles that go beyond the laws of humanity and religion, yet they complement many of the teachings of the main religions and philosophies of social ethics. Much has already been written about these spiritual principles or universal laws and of the harmonious flow of Universal Intelligence.

In synthesis, the spiritual principles that move the Universe are reflected in the organic flow of nature. You will observe that the sun shines on everything and everyone equally and unconditionally and that the rain falls over the earth without holding any expectations. The earth receives the gifts of sunshine and rain without asking for them and without exerting any efforts of its own to obtain them. Seeds slowly germinate and are nourished, under the right conditions, without anxious anticipation over their destiny, adaptable to the organic movement of nature, unattached to their development, surrendered to the process, simply growing with little effort, until they bear fruit, bestowing their bountiful gift onto the earth and all living creatures who nourish themselves from these gifts. The cycle continues, and each element reflects its authentic nature—each element of nature, flora and fauna, in perfect harmony, giving and receiving with least effort on the basis of their own intrinsic energy—giving, regenerating and recovering that which it surrenders and delivers unconditionally. They are inheritors of the rich and unlimited reservoir of the Universe which makes them participants in the perpetual circle of Love where Being and Giving unconditionally takes precedence over doing or receiving—where Being and Giving is life's inherent impulse—it is purpose in motion.

Akin to nature's reflection, we too originate from Creation's rich and abundant fountain spring, an infinite source that provides the fertile foundation to manifest all our desires. Universal Intelligence operates with perfect balance and harmony. By joining in nature's own rhythmic flow, we reach our goals with least effort. When we give to the world unconditionally that which we ourselves wish to receive, we automatically activate the energy of attraction to manifest what we desire. We attract into our lives the same energy state that is held in store by our intentions and our actions, and we deposit these in the Universe's bank which generates a return on our investment proportional to the same energy and intensity of whatsoever we deposit—this is otherwise known as karma or the physical law of action and reaction (Newton's third physical law of motion).

When we renounce our emphasis on the end result of our objectives, we take full pleasure in the actual process and path towards our goals. Paradoxically, with this newfound freedom of faith (trust), surrender and detachment—adaptable in the face of uncertainty and aligned with the harmonious flow of Universal Intelligence—our desires will be brought to fruition with effortless ease. When we surrender to the organizing power and intelligence of the Universe with trust, and as long as we do not violate the Universal Law of Love, our lives flow harmoniously with Divine Intelligence, bringing us abundance, joy, and personal fulfillment through the expression and convergence of our worldly (physical, external) and spiritual purpose both at an individual and collective level.

All of the spiritual principles are linked. When we deepen our practice of one principle, we deepen our practice of the others and as we incorporate them into our lives, we reach the illuminating revelation that they meld into each other and are in fact one Universal principal— the principal of Divine Love or Universal Love, which we will explore in more detail later.

We are the same Divine, dynamic energy that comprises Universal Intelligence—we are a microcosm of the Universe. Realigned with our Divine consciousness, we create and reflect in our lives that which we are, at the most expansive level of our Self.

By practicing and incorporating these universal principles (or Universal Law) in our daily living, we align with the source of Divine Creation, similarly reflecting the same abundance and well-being of the Universe in our lives. Aligned with spiritual law, we hold the key to the treasure of our Divine patrimony. However, when you violate or ignore these principles, the effects will not be life-supporting nor will they be compatible with the natural flow of the Universe. As such, the resulting effects will also not contribute to our own positive evolution or to the well-being of those around us.

You must, therefore, penetrate deeply and sincerely within to closely acknowledge your intentions before making any decision. For example, to help you clarify your true motivations ask yourself:

- ✓ What is my true intention?
- ✓ What emotion or energy (positive or negative) do I feel when I observe my intention?
- ✓ Is my intention aligned with my ego/false self or with my Higher Self/True Self?
- ✓ Is my intention congruent with the objective (of personal progress, happiness, etc.) that I desire?

This internal dialogue is a precursor to action. Always remember that your reactions, although they may not appear to be direct executions, are also "actions" that carry the energy of our intentions. Whatsoever the quality of our intentions when we react under any circumstance, we will produce results of the same magnetic affinity to the energy we radiate out into the world. It is therefore of equal importance to observe and take responsibility for our reactions to the stimuli presented by those with whom we interact and by the situations we face on a daily basis. A common saying is, how others treat you is their karma, and how you choose to react is yours. We can, therefore, ask ourselves, before responding verbally or physically:

- ✓ What effect do I wish to produce in my significant other (friend, colleague, etc.) by responding _____?
- ✓ Do I wish to hurt this person emotionally?
- ✓ Do I want to make this person feel guilty?
- ✓ What do I believe I gain by making him/her feel this way? What is my emotional payoff?
- ✓ Do I wish to prove that I am right?

It is invaluable that we live consciously aware of our intentions because the quality of their underlying energy will generate actions and consequences that activate the movement of the law of Karma or action and reaction (cause and effect) in our lives. There may be those who believe that our actions, what we do, is more important than our intentions. However, we cannot separate action from the intention and the energy that motivates it. The energy of your intention is the catalyzing agent of your actions in this world. It is the inner spark that ignites your motor to initiate your movement through life. Intention lives inside of you, in your silent inner space, before you pronounce a word, before you write and send an e-mail, before picking up your telephone to make a call, before choosing a career, before purchasing a car, before meeting a client, before negotiating a contract with a company. Intentions convey your motivations to acquire objectives in the external world yielding effects in the physical world.

My response to those individuals is that intention and action are one and the same. Intention and action are both energy, and energy is matter which may be comprised of different densities. Dense or solid energy is what we perceive in the physical world via our five senses (for example, our body is energy in solid form, and varies in density to what we hear, see, smell, taste, and touch). Intention is energy of unmanifested matter (not yet materialized in the physical world that we observe with our five senses), it is energy of a more subtle form, and action and its effects are the embodiment of the same energy in the physical world, the tangible world of our five senses where we physically observe actions and their consequences.

There may be occasions when one acts contrary to a given intention. Therefore, there are those who believe that what we do is more significant than our true intentions which usually remain inside of us, hidden from others. However, if we truly wish to transform the quality of our lives, it is not merely enough to conduct ourselves through life doing what we say we will do or complying with external expectations regardless of our personal desires and the suppression of any dark tendencies. Our intentions are a reflection of our state of consciousness and our energy. Therefore, although we may not act on the basis of a negative intention, the intention nonetheless exists as energy and resides internally. Even if it is not externalized at a given moment, the frequency and intensity of the energy reside within us. If we choose not to pay attention to diminishing it, it will eventually reflect itself and materialize its effects externally, if not on this occasion perhaps in another which triggers the same energy and emotions within us.

For example, if you do not get along with your neighbor because of constant friction, you may have the intention to get revenge. The violent intention was born of your state of unconsciousness. It is a negative energy grounded on anger and perhaps pride on your end. However, you decide to do nothing. If you neglect this feeling, the emotion will create strong roots in your store consciousness. These roots will be nourished from any incident or person that once again triggers this anger within you, even when it is no longer your neighbor. If you act on your intentions on this new occasion, it is because the energy of revenge, anger, and hostility already resided inside of you. Therefore, not acting on a given intention on certain occasions does not mean that the intention may not already have strong roots in your consciousness, of which without the attention of your Higher Self, they may potentially result in effects of unconsciousness and suffering in your life and your surroundings.

Some believe that good intentions have little significance as there are occasions when effects contrary to the original good intention result. However, circumstances such as these occur when we harbor more than one intention simultaneously, intentions that are inconsistent with our alleged conscious objective. There are conscious and unconscious intentions and desires which often remain suppressed and undisclosed to ourselves much less others. This means that when more than one intention exists in relation to a decision, the stronger intention, even when it is unconscious, becomes the dominant intention. This explains, for example, when a person seems to sabotage a relationship they claim they wish to save (or for example their employment position) and instead ruin or terminate it observing that the end result is, in fact, congruent with the dominant intention of the preferred result—what was truly unconsciously desired. We may be able to fool ourselves in terms of our false self, our ego, but we cannot fool the Universe in its wisdom. The organizing power of the Universe receives the information, intensity, and energy of our true intentions and desires. Our souls are an open book where nothing remains hidden from the Divine Intelligence of the Universe.

Just like seeds whose nuclei bear the intelligence to create flora of different varieties, your intentions carry all the information and energy to manifest fruits that are akin to the heart of your most intimate desires. As such, there must be a state of congruity between your intentions and your actions. This implies something greater than just suppressing negative intentions and acting contrary to them. It means that your intention is everything because your intention is the energy that drives all your present and future actions, it is what fuels your movement in this world, it is the fire that transforms your world and your reality. Your intentions are a reflection of yourself (your Self), of your energy and your values, a reflection of your state of consciousness, a portent of the fruits you will harvest.

5

KARMA: THE END AND THE MEANS ARE ONE

*The Universe is an echo which responds with
the same melody we confer on it.*

Our intentions are intimately interlaced with the principle of Karma or action and consequence, which is the same principle of giving and receiving that we observe circulating in nature. Karma, or cause and effect, is tantamount to the idea that we reap what we sow. Karma does not operate on the basis of judgment or punishment. Karma is an impersonal principle of the natural compensation of the Universe. It is a perfect accounting system where

The Wheel of Karma

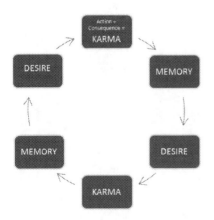

we receive in proportion to what we contribute to the Universe and where no debt ever goes unpaid.

The mechanism of karma operates in such way that our actions are archived in our memories, and these memories often generate desire which in turn triggers our actions once again. This cycle repeats itself creating actions and consequences, some positive and others negative. As long as our reality is solely comprised of the physical world of forms and we identify exclusively with our minds where our ego resides, the wheel of karma will continuously turn aligned with our false self. In this state of consciousness, our decisions are unconscious often resulting in negative karma and suffering.

Conversely, when our consciousness encompasses a reality that extends beyond the physical world of forms—an absolute, expansive reality where our sense of self is firmly anchored to our Higher Self—we will instead turn karma's wheel in alignment with our true essence. Grounded in this state of consciousness, we choose, make decisions and act consciously resulting in positive karma. When we choose from an awakened state, our Inner Master guides us towards evolutionary decisions that contribute to our happiness on both a personal and collective level.

We may either pay, transmute or transcend our karma. We pay our karmic debt when it is negative, when we are submerged in the unconsciousness of our ego. Innocent as to how the universal accounting system operates, we pay with suffering and hardships until we transform our reality and our consciousness. It is similar to consistently tripping and falling over the same pothole in the road until we learn to see it and avoid it when we encounter it. We transmute our karma when we learn lessons from our karma thereby transforming it into a positive experience that beneficially contributes to our spiritual and sometimes even material advancement, both individually and collectively. This is equivalent to forewarning others of the pothole on the road based on your experience and perhaps even devising a way to cover the pothole to prevent injury to others on the same path. Finally, we may transcend our karma when we expand our awareness to a state beyond the prison of our mind and ego. At this newfound level, you move beyond ego to your true essence and a state of Oneness. At this state, karma ceases to be "yours" altogether because you transcend to a point beyond the limited state that created the karmic episode, in other words, you transcend the false "you." You reach this level of Oneness consciousness through meditation, in the silent space that exists between each thought and each breath as described in chapter two.

Karma is an evolutionary mechanism available to us in the physical world of forms. As a tool, karma offers us the opportunity to choose our experiences, whether consciously or unconsciously, in order to learn and advance to a more expansive state of awareness, by either paying, transmuting or transcending our karmic debts. We always evolve, the difference is that so long as we choose on the basis of our ego, we are choosing unconsciously, as if asleep. At this stage, we will continue to pay most of our karma, so long as we do not awaken and abandon negative karmic cycles and patterns. Here, karma operates as if on automatic pilot, where we evolve slowly, tripping, falling and repeating many life lessons. However, when we are aligned with our true Self, our evolution is, by comparison, brisk and pleasant. In fact, the more connected we are to our Higher Self, the more we align our intentions with our actions and our life's purpose, which is known as Dharma in Sanskrit. At this stage, we are awake, conscious of our purpose and of our path, we choose each step in our evolution consciously grounded on the Divine Light of our spirit.

IDENTITY AND KARMIC INHERITANCE

Every decision produces effects on the lives of our descendants. This is what I call karmic inheritance. We inherit patterns from our proximate and distant ancestors which contribute to our spiritual evolution. In some cases, inherited patterns may be positive, while in others they may be negative. We should pay particular attention to these patterns, or karmic inheritance, as evolutionary tools but without fully identifying with the inheritance or pattern itself. If you remain rooted to your karmic inheritance and the negative patterns resulting from this legacy, you will end up believing and creating on the basis of these limitations. Karmic inheritances are valuable tools that present us with the parts in us that need to heal, they reveal to us where we need to learn and grow and reveal to us the portal to transcendence. Using this as a learning tool, we can rebalance the energy that our ancestors placed into circulation long before us, consequently resulting in the chain reaction of palpable effects in our current lives.

We are responsible for recognizing the negative pattern or effect of karmic inheritance at the root of our suffering. We are also responsible for choosing the energy frequency we wish to engender in order to rebalance our karmic debt. If we remain dormant, submerged in ego's unconsciousness, innocently unaware of our power to break any inherited negative patterns, we will undoubtedly act from a place of unconsciousness, mostly paying our inherited karma and perhaps even creating new negative karma that is compounded to our existing karmic debt, both personally and collectively.

If, for example, we choose to learn from our karmic inheritance by transmuting it, by this process alone we create new positive karma while we pay off our old karmic debts, balancing our account and our energy in a positive manner. If we transcend our karmic inheritance, we expand to an elevated state of consciousness where we liberate ourselves from karma completely. Herein lies a positive transformation at the spiritual level with both personal and collective benefits.

Personally, I identified the pattern that I was unconsciously trying to avoid (as I describe in the preface). I understood that I must neither restrict myself nor give any weight to external judgments. I chose to liberate myself from the karmic inheritance and the pattern rather than letting it oppress or hurt me, and rather than hiding it or defining myself in terms of it. I am firmly aware that I have the responsibility of choosing and defining my life's path. Aligned with my true Self, nothing invades me, I recognize who I am beyond any labels or external definitions, I remain centered on the authentic power of the Inner Master where my state of awareness reflects my true Self—I cultivate my inner path with every intention, thought, action, and word along my movement through this life's journey. This is my daily choice, and it is yours as well as you design and create with each step along your life's path.

For example, you may descend from a family of humble origins or perhaps descend from a family with a murky past or where an ancestor committed a crime, suffered from an addiction or destructive personal pattern, or otherwise made unsound decisions leading to an undesirable chain reaction of events. Sometimes there may even be vicious intergenerational cycles that we observe repeating themselves in some of our families. However, whatever your past or the negative patterns of your inherited karma, these do not define you nor do they predict the course of your life. Do not judge either your personal or your inherited past and do not fall prey to limiting yourself based on external judgments of past events on your timeline. Whatever we believe, we create. Do not imprison yourself with the chains of your past assuming that you are bound to an inevitable repetition of a vicious cycle. You define your own path and possess the power to liberate yourself from the fetters of past negative patterns. You choose your journey through life daily, with every intention, thought, action, and word, defining and creating your reality with each stride. Use your karmic inheritance and the negative patterns revealed to you as learning tools for your personal growth and spiritual transcendence.

Make choices from your Higher Self in order to evolve with the wisdom of your Inner Master, liberating yourself from the heavy burden of both your personal and inherited past. Cultivate your inner path daily transforming yourself each day and each moment. You always have the opportunity to choose as if for the first time and to be reborn with each decision in the present, which is the only moment that matters and which truly exists. Observe the patterns and karmic inheritance of your life without judgment and observe the manner in which they may have affected you, but do not remain there, navigating the surface of a limited and impermanent reality. It does not matter what your past or the past of your ancestors has been, do not blame the past nor the individual or collective states of consciousness that created the chain reaction of events that contributed to your present, instead embrace your past and your inheritance with tenderness and compassion in order to learn from them. Do not become an accomplice by labeling yourself with false notions of who you are not or by defining yourself in terms of your past. Delve deeply within your Self, cultivating your spiritual journey and penetrating into your Divine essence. Remain congruent and faithful to your Self and take responsibility for your transformation and for aligning yourself at each moment with the higher levels of positive frequency.

INTENTION AND KARMA

Our intentions are the prelude to an energy dynamic that we drive into motion through our actions. These intentions and actions create energy patterns that affect our personal lives as well as contribute to energy patterns that influence others at the collective level—at the level of our families, our neighborhoods, our cities, our culture, our ethnic group, our nation, our world. This is highly significant because our actions follow us our entire lives and beyond, leaving their trace and aftereffects among all who participate at the personal and collective level within our circle of influence, even after we have physically passed on. Regardless of how narrow our own circle of influence may appear to be, this is no less significant. This is evident on a smaller scale in our own families when we observe the progression and side-effects of karmic inheritance, like an unsuspecting chain reaction of dormant circumstances from the past, slowly unraveling itself into what has now apparently become our present state.

Within wider circles of influence, there is a more imposing burden of responsibility. For example, a person who, by the sheer power of his position as President of a nation identifies with his ego may, as a result of his prejudices and limited perception, cause irreparable damage to society and the world. For example, a leader who proposes to decimate a race or ethnicity he considers inferior (genocide), or who decides to expel from his nation individuals of a different nationality or culture due to characteristics he devalues, or a leader who targets people and nations of a different culture or religion through violent terrorist acts.

Unfortunately, human history is still being plagued to this day by many of these examples. Our leaders have many followers, and their perceptions, intentions, thoughts, words and actions are by no means static. They exercise great influence over their followers with the power to incite violence, fear, intolerance, and destruction, or conversely, the power to guide their followers towards harmony, unity, understanding, and peace.

The energy of our intentions impels our actions and continue us daily through every one of our interactions. Like a pebble flung into a placid lake, where waves of concentric circles slowly expand and extend outward, the amplitude of its reach proportional to the size of the stone and the momentum used to cast it into the water. We are responsible for what we bestow as our gift to the world each day because every action and its effects influence us and invade the lives of everyone else around us, directly and indirectly. Our decisions are interwoven in an intricate and extensive web that encompasses the entire world. It can be said that our intentions travel around the world and expand throughout the Universe.

What this means is that our most precious gift is not material. Our most invaluable gift to ourselves and others and the world is the gift of actions grounded in Understanding, Compassion, Love that is inclusive, and Peace, all of which guarantee bountiful fruits to be harvested by all participants and recipients. Material gifts do not guarantee the same rewards because they lack intrinsic value. Material things and money can never equate to words or actions stemming from clear intentions based on kindness, compassion, peace and Love.

Where does this chain reaction of intentions and actions that circulate the world initiate? The answer is not that significant. In reality, there is no beginning and no end, just like a circle in perpetual motion. Measuring the initial action and its effect is impossible. This phenomenon is described in quantum physics which finds its complementary parallel in mysticism. As demonstrated by Bell's Theorem, there are no local independent events; the Universe is interconnected, interdependent, and inseparable. This theorem supports traditions of mysticism and teachings of Buddhism which describe that we inter-are, that we are interconnected and interdependent and that no thing or no one has an individualized, independent or separate nature from everything else that exists.[1]

It is therefore important to become consciously aware of what we initiate daily through the energy of our intentions and decisions, assuming full responsibility for our participation in the co-creation of our lives at the individual level as well as for our collective engagement in the co-creation of our world.

We are all intimately interlaced, participating daily in a drama that has no written script, improvising both consciously and unconsciously before the actions and reactions of our ensemble cast in this stage show called Life. We are co-responsible in the co-creation of our world and when we awaken to this truth, we are able to appreciate the importance of radiating positive energy through our words and thoughts and we value the significance of acting constructively in Life which is but one shared experience with our brothers and sisters, with all of our co-participants in this world and this Universe.

To awaken to this state of consciousness translates to Being and giving that which one wishes to experience and receive from life and the Universe. We do not attract what we want from the Universe but what we ARE based on our state of awareness. As Einstein once stated, "We cannot solve our problems with the same thinking we used when we created them." Therefore, in order to transform our experience of life, we must transform the quality of our intentions, our perceptions, our thoughts, our words, and our actions, we must, in other words, transform our state of consciousness.

Once we become conscious that we attract what we are—attracting the same energy that we radiate with our intentions, thoughts, and actions—we begin our journey towards true freedom. By becoming consciously aware that we, in fact, create our own experiences, that we alone are fully responsible for the old, negative patterns that have held us back, we come to the realization that full responsibility also means that we exercise the power to adopt new, positive patterns that liberate us from our self-imposed emotional prisons and which attract the abundance and happiness that we have always desired and yet often struggled to obtain.

Undoubtedly, you created the reflection of the world that you see around you, therefore, with the same power and means by which you created it, you can also un-create it. The world does not change for us. The world cannot change because this world's "reality," as we perceive it, is in actuality an effect, and the cause of that effect, which we experience as reality or our subjective experience of the world, is your thoughts, and the thoughts of all of our co-participants in this lifetime. Therefore, responsibility for change lies in oneself—in you, in me, in us.

If we see and experience what we do not like, who is responsible if not oneself? Recognizing the cause of what we experience and realizing that the cause lies in our own hands is liberating, but at the same time, it carries the weight of total responsibility. It is our individual and collective responsibility to change the cause—our thoughts and perceptions—in order to free ourselves from old patterns that create obstacles for our growth and development, and which block the expansion of our consciousness (awareness) and of our reconnection with the true states of Love and Happiness. By changing the quality of our perceptions, our thoughts, our words and our actions, we propel the change we wish to see and experience around us and throughout the entire world. We are creators, and we create on the basis of our consciousness, based on our intentions and our will. We create in terms of what we believe, and we project these same beliefs onto the world which in turn materialize into the world we see and experience daily, comparable to what one sees reflected in a high definition mirror.

MINDFULNESS

So long as we conduct ourselves through life thinking that "the end justifies the means," as Nicolo Machiavelli expressed in The Prince, we will remain blindfolded, guided and imprisoned by our egos. To act on the basis of this rule is to not know one's true essence and that the Universe unfolds in terms of spiritual principles or laws. The end and the means are not independent in and of themselves; they are not separate elements. The end and the means are the same as they are one and oneself. When you recognize that the end and the means are one and oneself, because they originate from you and share your same energy, you begin to consciously contemplate your intentions, words, and actions with the same tender care of a gardener for her rosebush. This state of conscious contemplation is called mindfulness. Here you start to cultivate the positive seeds of that which you desire to flourish in your own life and in your environment.

Mindfulness is the exercise of conscious contemplation with detachment and nonjudgment. It entails observation without the need to qualify, interpret or append anything to our observations. Mindfulness, as described in Buddhist teachings, involves observation without evaluating, analyzing or judging what we observe. It is a calm and awakened presence before each moment's unfolding, gently and nonjudgmentally accepting everything that transpires within and outside of oneself. In this state of presence, you experience the union of body, mind, and spirit. It is the act of contemplating all of your intentions, emotions and life events with an awakened or alert consciousness, without chastising yourself for whatever you dislike in yourself and without blaming others for their unconscious actions.

Mindfulness also allows you to water and strengthen the roots of all the positive intentions and emotions that reside in your store consciousness, such as kindness, compassion, peace, and love. Mindfulness allows you to center yourself in order to observe your inner impulses with greater clarity and wisdom and helps shift your state of awareness to higher ground, contributing to your spiritual development within your worldly existence.

How does one begin? First, with the intention that maintaining this mindful state will be your new priority. Before making any decision or reacting to any stimuli, you remind yourself of your commitment to liberate yourself from suffering and expand to a state of spiritual and emotional wholeness. You begin by acknowledging all of your personal thoughts and perceptions on life that have trapped you in the prison of what appears to be a never-ending negative cycle. For example, our perceptions are subjective, and they often reflect our prejudices, our ignorance, our anger, our arrogance, our desires, and attachments, all of which causes much suffering. When you delve deeply into the nature of your perceptions, you will begin to cultivate perceptions and thoughts of better quality. Your personal point of view is not the truth nor is it the only way to perceive things; it is simply one of many ways in which to understand life and view the many situations you encounter daily. Each time a negative perception or thought arises, remind yourself that it is simply a self-created subjective judgment and that you hold power to transform the quality of these perceptions and thoughts with the positive energy of love, compassion, understanding, and peace.

GUIDE FOR MINDFUL RIGHT ACTION

Mindfulness also serves as a valuable guide for improving the quality of our actions. When you incorporate mindfulness in all your decisions, you experience that, by making conscious choices which avoid the hardships associated with negative karma at the individual and collective levels, suffering is greatly diminished. By becoming mindful of the quality of your actions, you begin to enjoy the bounty of happiness and well-being at the level of your body, mind, and spirit.

The Buddhist tradition offers a lovely guide that allows us to cultivate right action. Buddhism is not a religion but a guide for increasing well-being and alleviating suffering in the physical world. It provides the ethics of good living at both the personal and collective level, and the teachings complement the principles of the main religious traditions. The Five Mindfulness Trainings, as described in Buddhist teachings are:

1- Reverence for Life—Nonviolence
2- Generosity
3- Sexual Responsibility
4- Right Speech
5- Mindful Consumption

REVERENCE FOR LIFE

Reverence for life means not killing or exercising violence not just in terms of our actions but also in terms of our intentions, thoughts, and words. It implies valuing life in all its expressions, in terms of all sentient beings with whom we share this world—humans, flora, fauna.

It means not practicing violence towards oneself with negative decisions or patterns that contribute to our self-destruction by what we consume, by what we think of ourselves, of others and the world. Reverence for life means to value life as one, which we share with all sentient beings as one single thread that flows through each one of us equally.

GENEROSITY

Generosity means sharing not just at the material level, but also by giving of oneself, giving our attention and presence to those who need us. It means giving that which promotes life, love, compassion and peace. It implies not stealing or defrauding nor supporting anyone who seeks economic gain by deceiving humankind.

SEXUAL RESPONSIBILITY

Sexual responsibility refers to not sustaining sexual relations without love or without an authentic commitment as a couple. It means avoiding sexual compulsion, promiscuity, and adultery. It means avoiding the sexual exploitation of vulnerable individuals such as children and adolescents, among others. Exercising sexual responsibility protects us at the individual, family, and societal levels.

RIGHT SPEECH

Right speech means exercising utmost care with our words both verbally and in writing. I can personally attest that this has been one of the most profound and fruitful lessons for me both on a personal and professional level, providing me with immediate benefits. Right speech means expressing yourself truthfully, with gentleness and kindness, under all circumstances especially when faced with the most difficult situations. In Chapter 3 we explored the importance of our intentions. Right speech is much more than simply measuring your words before expressing yourself. Right speech implies an intimate congruence between your intentions and your communication. Our words are very powerful because they carry the energy of our intentions and with it the ability to cause injury and damage or conversely, the ability to heal, promote peace, and love. It is important to be mindful of our intentions before expressing ourselves through any medium, be it in person, over the telephone, in written form or on social networks. Today's technology affords us the ability to communicate with each other around the world in seconds. With a "click" of your finger, you can transmit your energy, your intentions, and your point of view to the entire world. You share yourself with the interconnected web of our external world and with it, you place into circulation your gift to the world. This is an impressive advancement but one that involves great responsibility.

If you are to write a letter or send an e-mail, it is best to do so in a state of mindfulness, especially if you are communicating with someone that you dislike, or when you require responding to a complex situation, one that may perhaps trigger negative emotions in you. For example, right speech means practicing communication that is free of prejudice and aggression. It is communication that is free of lies, pride, sarcasm, anger or any expression intended to attack, hurt or stimulate toxic emotions. When you exercise right speech, you are grounded in truth, you are objective and diplomatic, and the intentions that impel your words seek to heal emotional wounds, seek cooperation, seek mutual understanding at the deepest level of Self, and seek solutions to problems that are peaceful and compassionate.

When your intentions are positive, the energy supporting your communication is rooted in the authentic power of your Higher Self. The recipient of your communication will receive the energy and the underlying message of your intention and will respond in light of the same frequency that you initiated. When confronted by difficult situations, right speech yields immediate effects and we place into circulation the same energy we wish to receive in our lives. Before picking up your phone, before sending a text or e-mail, or clicking to post your next message on social networks ask yourself, what is my intention with this communication? Will my words contribute to contaminating or nourishing this world? If your intention does not contribute to anything constructive or is not altogether clear, delay your communication until you clear your mind, calm your body and spirit and are able to communicate positively. Otherwise, you will be hurting not just the recipient but yourself in the process.

MINDFUL CONSUMPTION

Being mindful of what we consume does not only refer to the consumption of food but to everything that we consume in varying forms. The Buddha described four types of nutriments that we subject ourselves to continuously: (i) Nutrition—food/drink, (ii) Consumption through our five senses, (iii) Intention or personal will, and (iv) Consciousness

(i) NUTRITION

When we nourish our bodies we should choose nourishment that is wholesome and free of toxins. It implies avoiding or eliminating foods, drinks or other consumptions that do not contribute to a healthy body, mind, and spirit such as, alcohol, tobacco or cigarettes, and drugs which are toxic to our lungs, liver, and brain. Their effects are toxic to our loved ones also, both directly and indirectly because of the physical, and emotional suffering caused to our families and our society who suffer because of our unconscious consumption.

Realistically, we do not live in a Buddhist monastery, which means that if you drink socially, you will not likely stop drinking altogether. The important point to apply in our secular lives is to practice mindfulness in terms of how and what we consume, to delve deeply into what factors motivate our drinking, smoking, etc., and to recognize whether you depend on drinking or other consumption to feel happy or emotionally stable and become conscious of the effects of your use. For example, if you become drunk every time you drink, or your consumption interferes with your personal relationships and your work, or if you notice that unless you have those couple of drinks daily or weekly you do not feel quite well, your consumption is likely toxic at a personal, family and collective level. It means that you probably depend on this consumption to fill an emotional void or are using it as a form of escapism from the present moment. Eliminating it completely would be ideal and diminishing it would also be highly beneficial. Maintaining your health through a mindful and balanced consumption will protect your health on an individual, family, and collective level.

(ii) CONSUMPTION THROUGH OUR FIVE SENSES

We are constantly also consuming through our five senses. We consume the TV programs we choose to watch individually, with our families and friends. We consume books, magazines, music, games and conversations. When the content of what we consume is violent or contributes to negative criticism, anger, and sexual irresponsibility or is otherwise toxic, it does not contribute to a healthy mind, body and spirit. It is important to observe the content of what we consume and avoid that which negatively affects or distracts us from our spiritual growth and negatively influences our families and our society.

I recommend the occasional exercise of a "diet" where we avoid all distracting and toxic consumption in order to bring lightness to our mind, emotions and spirit. For example, you may practice a "technological diet" by shutting off your electronic gadgets, your TV, tablets, and cell phones and disconnecting from social networks for one hour or one whole day to detox from stimuli that causes distraction and turbulence in your mind. Unplugging helps to calm you, allows you to rediscover your true essence and foments positive thoughts that nourish your intentions and your actions. Connecting with your internal space and expanding your spiritual practice becomes more difficult when you are constantly receiving toxic and distracting stimuli.

If we evaluate the messages and stimuli that TV presents us with, for example, we will see that the majority is directed to strengthening our ego. Commercials, for the most part, make us believe that we need to buy material things to raise our social status or increase our happiness, or that we need to buy products that improve our appearance to feel better about ourselves. Although there are exceptions, the majority of popular programs are distractions that contribute little value to our personal and spiritual growth and mainly serve as a form of escapism from the present moment.

The more we connect with this media, the more we connect with the collective unconsciousness. It is unconsciousness because we think and act without knowing what we are doing, living as if "plugged-in" to an external reality that we have accepted without questioning it, like in the movie *The Matrix* (Wachowski, 1999). Fully connecting to social media and networks, the internet, games, and TV distract us from reconnecting with the internal space of our true Self which is the unlimited source of true abundance and Happiness.

In the physical world of forms the ego is king. We live in a system that nourishes and sustains itself from our egoistic unconsciousness. We live in a multimillion dollar, commercialized system that exists on the basis of supplying the insatiable desires and false needs of the ego. We are constantly being sold the idea that we can fill our inner void with luxury brands, automobiles, the latest technological gadgets, beauty and anti-aging products that promise youth and happiness and the false, implicit promise of augmenting our aggregate value. To such a system it is inconvenient that we awaken from the unconsciousness of our ego and that we align instead with the wisdom of our true essence. When we awaken from the unconsciousness of the ego, the system is unable to control, exploit, manipulate or imprison us, and it is unable to sell us the illusion of false value and ephemeral happiness. When we awaken to a state of pure consciousness, beyond ego, we become rooted in the authentic power of our Higher Self, we recognize our intrinsic value, and we realize that we are whole, thereby transforming the quality of our human experience. We see the light of truth. We are free.

(iii) INTENTION, PERSONAL WILL OR VOLITION

Our intentions and volition also nourish us. Our intentions and our will are a reflection of what we value and desire. It is according to our intention or will that we infuse with energy all that we value and wish to manifest in our lives. For example, if an individual's objective is to earn the maximum amount of money irrespective of what is required to that end, whether it be illegal or unethical, he will persist until he reaches his aim. His mind and energy will remain fixed, day and night even in his dream state, to create the means to his end. This individual will consume on the basis of this energy and this in turn will nourish his consciousness and everything he executes with the intensity of his volition to reach his goal. If this person believes that money is the only thing that will provide him with happiness and, hypothetically, has no remorse in trafficking drugs or becoming a trained hitman, his will/volition would in fact be a toxic consumption that contributes to his own suffering, the suffering of his family and the suffering of our society. If we are mindful of our intentions and cultivate wholesome intentions that instead contribute to our expansion and freedom from suffering, we will soon become aware that material things, although pleasurable, do not provide us with a permanent state of happiness. By cultivating intentions that support reverence to life, love, peace, and compassion, we will nourish our will and our individual consciousness with the seeds of true well-being for ourselves, our families, and the collective consciousness.

(iv) CONSCIOUSNESS

Consciousness is the fourth type of nourishment and is composed of all of our roots comprised of the emotions, thoughts, and actions that we have cultivated and strengthened throughout our lives. These, in turn, are formed from our past, from the perceptions that we have inherited from our families as well as assimilated from the collective consciousness, such as our society, our culture, and our nation, among others. Our thoughts, words, actions, and everything else we ingest daily, continuously nourish our consciousness. Whatever we value and focus our attention on grows and expands contributing to the formation of our state of awareness. It is therefore important to mindfully nourish our consciousness with wholesome values that protect us as individuals and as a society. For example, rather than feed our consciousness with hatred, lust, greed or envy we may instead choose mindfully to nourish ourselves daily with love, a sense of oneness, peace, compassion, and joy for life.

In Buddhist teachings, mindfulness is an integral part of every action that is undertaken and in how one carries oneself through life's journey in order to obtain freedom from suffering and cultivate well-being at the personal and collective levels. A symbol which I love and which reminds me of this teaching is the image of an eye at the center of the palm of a hand. This symbol is frequently seen in deities of Tibetan, Chinese, Japanese, Korean, and Vietnamese temples. The eye symbolizes understanding and insight which nourish mindfulness. The hand symbolizes our actions. In my personal interpretation, each finger symbolizes the Five Mindfulness Trainings—this helps me keep them present each time I look at the palm of my hand. The image is a gentle reminder that each time you carry yourself forward in life through your actions, you will do so with the higher vision of your soul's enlightened state and with the conscious depth of mindful presence. With this practice, you will be offering, from your hand to others, the gift of your finest actions, and whatsoever you touch will flower, leaving behind the sweet balsam of your noble right actions.

PEACE PRAYER OF ST. FRANCIS

The Catholic tradition also offers us a beautiful guide for cultivating good intentions and actions, the prayer of Saint Francis of Assisi also known as the Peace Prayer of St. Francis. Saint Francis's teaching is equivalent to a formula of spiritual alchemy because it transforms hate, doubt, hopelessness and sadness into love, faith, hope, and joy. It is the chemistry that manifests the field of Divine Consciousness right here on earth. By practicing this level of mindfulness, our intentions, our actions, and our lives are transformed by the authentic power of the Universe thereby manifesting Paradise on Earth in our lives and our environment. During my childhood and adolescence, I attended Catholic school and was familiar with Saint Francis's prayer, but until most recently, I had not fully contemplated and absorbed the depth, wisdom, and energy of the words. The prayer reads:

PRAYER OF SAINT FRANCIS OF ASSISI

Lord, make me an instrument of your peace;
Where there is hatred, let me sow love;
Where there is injury, let me sow pardon;
Where there is doubt, faith;
Where there is despair, hope;
Where there is darkness, light;
Where there is sadness, joy.

Oh Divine Master,
Grant that I may not so much seek
To be consoled as to console;
To be understood as to understand;
To be loved as to love;
For it is in giving that we receive;
It is in pardoning that we are pardoned;
And it is in dying that we are born to eternal life.

This prayer is a guide that incorporates all of the spiritual principles discussed in the third chapter. It begins with the premise that we derive from a Divine source, what some call God, Pure Consciousness, Divine Intelligence, Undifferentiated Consciousness, Tao, among others, and which is the fountain head of unlimited resources. When we align with this field within our human experience, which is our true essence at the purest state, we become vessels who give birth to the same light of Divine Consciousness through our actions in the physical world. Aligned to this Divine energy, we understand that we must initiate the action of giving in order to place into circulation that which we desire and wish to manifest in our own lives. The key is that we cannot be passive and wait to receive. It is by giving that one receives, not the other way around. We must first sow peace, love, faith, hope, light and joy in order to reap a rich harvest. We must first console, forgive and love rather than expect to be comforted, forgiven and loved in return. We must become the change we wish to experience in our world and in this way turn the wheel of positive karma in our lives to derive the most fruitful rewards that benefit us and our world. When you proceed in this manner, little effort is required to obtain wholesome results because, by remaining authentic to your nature and aligned with Divine Intelligence, you radiate an energy that envelops everyone and everything positively and everything you render is at one with the harmonious flow of nature and of the Universe. The positive intentions of St. Francis's prayer are a gentle reminder of the importance of the energy which propels our actions in order to manifest everything we contribute to this world. St. Francis exposes a state of consciousness that is contrary to the characteristic attachment of ego, describing instead a state of unconditional selflessness and dedication to our Divine source, recognizing that dying in oneself, which is in fact the disintegration of the ego, Life Eternal is obtained, which is the expansive consciousness of the Higher Self, aligned to Infinite Intelligence, Divine or Pure Consciousness. Finally, the state of consciousness towards which St. Francis is guiding us reveals a life purpose where spirituality and being of service to others becomes a priority, it becomes the daily path we undertake through all our interactions, which is the same as our life's Dharma in Sanskrit. In fact, St. Francis guides us towards one universal principle that encompasses everything—Universal Love or Divine Love.

Through the practice of the spiritual principles that underlie the natural flow of the Universe and by using the words of the Buddha and St. Francis as signposts, we become the vehicles through which un-manifested Divinity becomes manifest in the physical world of forms. We become true alchemists, materializing a bounty of peace and light throughout our life's journey in this material existence we so happen to embody.

Each one of us is a musical chord in the One Song of our Universal Symphony. Be mindful in maintaining your tone pure, firm, harmonious, and clear that it may be attuned to the natural and Divine harmony of the Universe. When you align yourself to your true essence, you will experience the illuminating reality that your life flows fully and effortlessly with the natural rhythm of the Universe. In this state of consciousness, you will delight in the musical harmony of the Universe reflected in your own life, because just like an echo, the universe responds with the same melody that you confer on it.

6

ACCEPTANCE AND RESPONSIBILITY

When you accept life without resistance,
you assume responsibility for transforming
your reality, aligning yourself with the
intelligent flow of the Universe.

THE NEGATIVE ROLE OF GUILT

No one is responsible for the personal reality we live. If we wish our lives, our environment, and our reality to change, we, at the individual level, are the only ones responsible for initiating the changes required to reach this end. Neither the world nor others change to accommodate us and our needs. No matter how much we would like or expect for external changes to take place and magically fix our lives, we cannot control external factors or behavior but we can certainly modify our own and with it, our experience of the world.

We may observe that when things do not turn out as expected or when people do not behave as one hopes, we impose blame on the person, group or situation that caused us injury or emotional unease. We live in the shadow of what I denominate a human culture of guilt were blame, guilt, and remorse play an active role. Since childhood, we have been indoctrinated with the culture of blame and remorse. As children, many of us may have experienced moments where adult caretakers and educators used guilt as a device to control and modify our behavior. Some of us may have heard phrases such as:

"Don't do that, that's bad! Good
children don't do that!"

"If you behave badly, God will become sad
and cry!" (or become angry and punish you.)

With our limited capacity as children, this technique worked perfectly well for our parents to obtain the stellar behavior they expected from us. Having learned this as children, we internalized this pattern, either consciously or unconsciously, acquiring it as a tool for our day to day dealings in life. We learn early on that if we cast blame on others, we can manipulate and attempt to control situations and the behavior of others.

We may observe the extreme example of guilt's important role in the litigious culture of the U.S., where Civil lawsuits are a million dollar operation, and money is the end goal. In my legal profession, it is common to see cases where individuals seek to abuse the system and where greed is largely at play, often seeing alleged victims preying on individuals or companies aiming to win a million dollar lawsuit for claimed injuries. I am in no way opposed to lawsuits and our judicial system which seek to compensate injured parties; the point is that it illustrates the monetization of guilt and injury or damage at its extreme, where the monetary valuation obtained and imposed as punishment is proportional to the degree of culpability and harm caused. I remember that long before I decided to become an attorney, I met a real estate agent who was married to a lawyer. In almost all of her conversations, she invoked the power of the lawsuit as her standard go-to remedy to resolve any given issue or dispute against individuals or entities. In terms of our penal system, capital punishment is the most extreme application of punishment which is currently applied in 31 states in the U.S. The heightened degree of significance we afford blame, guilt, and retribution in proportion to harm, is deeply rooted in our consciousness.

Although guilt may be a conventional tool and its effects likely result beneficial at the material level, guilt never produces positive results at the spiritual level. Feeling and imposing guilt on oneself, as well as on others, is a negative, destructive emotion. The feeling of guilt strengthens our ego.

"IT IS NEVER MY FAULT": THE BLAME GAME

Our ego is actively involved when we impose guilt on others. If another is to blame, it means that one is right, which makes the other party wrong. Placing blame on others implies a level of superiority over the opposing party—it means living on the defensive with an impulse to distinguish "oneself" from "others." Placing blame on others for a situation or event involves resistance to the manner in which external events develop and suggests an evasion of personal responsibility for our actions and perceptions which contribute to the circumstances that unfold in our lives. A funny anecdote helps illustrate the point. One Friday, after a long and exhausting work day, I closed my office at the scheduled time happy to go home to rest. As I walk towards my car, I see one of my clients from a distance. As soon as she sees me, she walks briskly towards me and says, "I tried to get here on time but I went home first after work, and there was heavy traffic getting here. It was impossible for me to get here earlier!" This client did not have an appointment with me and never called in advance to tell me she was stopping by that same day. I told her I was sorry, as I had unfortunately already closed and she would have to come back the next day during my scheduled office hours. The client did not wish to come in the next day because she knew that Saturdays are the busiest day at the office, but she agreed to come back anyway. The following day when we met, she says to me sadly, "If you had met with me yesterday, I wouldn't have crashed my car today." I could not believe it! She was blaming me for ramming her car against a beam as she backed up to park in front of my office! "Now I'll have to fix my car. The damage looks so bad," she says to me, downtrodden. All I could do was console her and try my best to help her compassionately with matters bringing her to my office. However, I stored her reaction in my memory, and I giggled amusedly to myself each time I revisited the incident, because of the humor and sheer innocence of her conjecture. In fact, it still makes me chuckle, and I value the lesson provided by the episode.

So long as you find someone to blame for whatever happens to you or for what you feel, you believe to have liberated yourself from responsibility over a given situation. You erroneously believe yourself to be at an advantage over the guilty party. As long as you are "innocent" you are simply the victim, and the guilty party is the "villain." You believe to have identified the main characters in the age-old drama of "good vs. evil," and we all know that the good always triumphs against the bad. The ego loves playing this game of casting blame, of complaining, of identifying its enemies and those responsible for its suffering.

"IT'S ALWAYS MY FAULT": THE GAME OF BLAMING ONESELF

There are individuals who, rather than blame others, consistently find fault in themselves, feeling guilt and remorse for any unpleasant situation, no matter how insignificant. I am not speaking of an occasional feeling of guilt but a state of consciousness equivalent to a constant emotional self-flagellation. At its most extreme, this emotion is undoubtedly negative and is a heavy burden for those who are constantly punishing themselves. This state of consciousness is often associated with guilt over your personal past and your karmic inheritance. Individuals at this state often take on a victim identity where they judge, condemn, and invalidate themselves regularly because they are unaware of the intrinsic value of their True Self. At this state, individuals emanate a low-frequency energy, often provoking the same type of punishment from others which they innocently believe to deserve. Individuals who suffer from a great sense of guilt are more likely to suffer from ailments and are often "accident" prone. This inner state of severe guilt is cruelty and violence to oneself. It is a negative and destructive pattern which blocks love, health, happiness and peace from our lives and contributes nothing to nourish our personal growth.

In order to liberate ourselves from suffering, it is imperative to break the pattern of personal guilt. Instead of remaining stagnant within this destructive pattern, one must bravely assume the responsibility of aligning oneself with a higher, positive frequency and seek personal transformation. The major spiritual philosophies teach and espouse the practice of nonjudgment, nonviolence, and unconditional love for humankind. In this same manner, we must apply these teachings to ourselves. The key to unlocking this self-imposed prison is to remind ourselves that we are perfect beings at the spiritual level which is our core. We must understand that we are not guilty, we are innocent beings negatively programmed by the ego (false "self") as well as programmed with the illusory reality that the material world of forms has "sold" us. We must perceive our ego, and the victim identity with which it identifies, with compassion whenever we impose guilt on ourselves and against others with severity. At such moments, we should embrace ourselves with the same tenderness with which a mother embraces her innocent child, offering it deep understanding and unconditional love, reminding the child of how precious and loved she truly is. By reconnecting with our inner Self, we align ourselves with our true nature where fear and guilt disappear and are instead replaced by the stability of our authentic power, which is none other than the innocent wisdom of our Higher Self and the inclusive oneness of Universal Love.

ESCAPING FROM THE PATTERN OF GUILT

Identifying ourselves as victims is yet another identity the ego loves to adopt. Everything with which we identify is ego, but so long as we think of ourselves as victims, we will retain the role of passive participants on life's stage. Life on these terms is characterized by non-acceptance or resistance to the unfolding of life events as well as by the act of not assuming personal responsibility for our perceptions and the manner in which we choose to confront unpleasant circumstances along our life's journey. The issue is that we happily accept everything that we find to be pleasing and contributes to ease and comfort in our lives, but it is an entirely different story when we face challenging and uncomfortable situations in our lives. Non-acceptance of events as they are, and as they arise, is an act of resistance to life itself and to the natural unfolding of the Universe, which is an intricate chain that links each and every moment we are living. Resistance before life's complex situations is like navigating a river on a canoe, paddling upstream against the wind's current. Resisting what "is" is counterproductive. Non-acceptance and resistance is draining, stressful and results in most of our suffering.

We create our own reality. Numerous experiments in quantum physics reveal to us that there is no independent reality outside the observer. The observer and whatsoever is observed are part of the same system where the object of observation is in fact affected and created by the observer. Taking this to practical application in our own lives, we can see that each one of us holds the personal responsibility for changing our perceptions, our thoughts and the frequency with which we connect to shape our reality.

Each frequency presents us with a different picture. By changing the frequency we tune into, we observe that what was once real or true no longer is. Each frequency level gives rise to a different quality of thoughts and reality. As such, we create our own reality based on the frequency with which we choose to align. For example, we can opt to align ourselves with low-frequency energies dominated by hate, resentment, envy, guilt and fear or we can instead choose to align ourselves with the higher energy frequencies of courage, acceptance, understanding, compassion, love and peace.

There are studies and experiments that describe in detail the different levels of energy frequencies associated with our emotions which in turn correspond to the various states of consciousness (David R. Hawkins, 1995, 2012). There are parallels between these studies and Eastern spiritual traditions, such as in acupuncture, yoga, tai chi, among others, that describe the body's energy centers (Chakras), the meridians of the energetic body, the emotions associated with each point, and the importance of unblocking negative energy contributing to the easeful flow of energy for optimum physical, mental and spiritual health.

In synthesis, everything emits energy, whether positive or negative, and this energy can be measured and calibrated to discover its essence and truth (David R. Hawkins, 1995, 2012). The varying energy frequencies create energy patterns or different consciousness levels which in turn attract energy patterns of the same affinity. In his studies and experiments, Hawkins discovered a method to calibrate the energy we emit through Kinesiology,[2] creating a "Map of Consciousness" where, for each energy level calibrated, a given value was obtained to arrive at a linear logarithmic scale of energetic power that ascends from 1-1000.[3] Dr. Hawkins has been a pioneer in the field of consciousness studies. I highly recommend his works to anyone seeking to deepen their understanding and knowledge within the vast and rich terrain of consciousness.

Intuitively, we have known that we emit energy and surely on one or more occasions we have experienced sensing negative or positive energy emitted by another individual or a given environ. Investigations and studies simply confirm with science and mathematics what we have inherently known and complement the wisdom of Eastern traditions. Low-frequency energy is what we call negative, and high-frequency energy is what we call positive.

Each level of energy presents us with a different reality, with a different human experience and even a different concept of God. When we internalize the value of these studies at the personal and collective level, we awaken to the authentic and creative empowerment of our Higher Self which resides within and accompanies us always. We become aware that we possess the tools to create our own reality, to improve the quality of our human experience and to expand our consciousness at the spiritual level where freedom from suffering is available.

How does one ascend on the energy scale? In order to connect with the higher frequencies of energy and experience immediate change in our quality of life, we must first, and most importantly, reach the state of acceptance. At this frequency or state of consciousness, we stop blaming others for the painful and unpleasant situations of our lives that have resulted from our past as well as from our present. Here, we take full responsibility for our actions and omissions in life. We stop pointing our fingers in search of the "villains" of our personal drama in order to justify our lives, our negative emotions and the negative patterns to which we are often unconsciously attached and which no longer serve us. The act of seeking justifications, of complaining, and of blaming the outside world for whatever is "done" to us is one more erroneous ego identification, a vulnerable and weak position based on a passive victim identity assumed in life, an identity which often seeks pity, empathy and protection from others. I remind you that the ego is a false "I" or false "self". It seeks identification with any label or energy that maintains its sense of self alive. Our ego fears death and fears disappearing because it believes to "be" who we are. The ego resists everything that appears to threaten its existence and its sense of self. The ego nourishes and strengthens itself from the drama of our lives and from the stories we create and believe about ourselves and the world in which we live.

As long as we connect to negative frequencies and blame ourselves and others for the situations we face, we will be shirking our personal responsibility and negating our true, authentic power as creative beings, as well as denying our responsibility for reconnecting with the Inner Light of our Higher Self which enlightens and guides us with wisdom. When connected to lower or negative frequencies (such as shame, fear, anger, and pride) the ego and a narrative of unconsciousness dominate which contribute nothing positive towards our growth and spiritual transcendence. At these inferior energy levels, we primarily believe in our material needs and our survival in the material world. The needs of what is "I," "me," or "mine" is the priority. At these levels, our reality is fragmented and we are unable to see beyond duality; everything in this limited perception of reality moves in terms of opposites, in terms of separation between "I" and "all others," or "us" vs. "them," thoughts of loss vs. gain and the constant struggle against "evil" and darkness.

When we connect to higher or positive frequencies—for example, courage, acceptance, compassion, love, peace, and spiritual transcendence or Enlightenment, which is the highest vibrational frequency—we operate from the authentic power center of our True or Higher Self. At these levels, we primarily believe in Pure Consciousness as our true Self, and the act of awakening and expanding our state of consciousness to the highest states becomes our top priority and reality, where Love, Peace, and freedom from suffering and from the prison of our ego operate.

Within our human experience, it is natural to fluctuate between energy frequencies on different occasions at the various stages of our lives. The important thing is to know that we are responsible for the frequency or energy with which we choose to align at any given moment. One does not suggest that aligning with levels where the ego dominates is "bad," but one will likely notice that by only focusing on our material needs and connected to inferior energy frequencies, we experience the adverse effects of our ego and with it, our suffering. At the superior levels of energy and of expanded consciousness, we live in a state of surrender and non-resistance before life, trusting in Divine Order where we manifest fruits of the same frequency, creating a reality that is full in its wholeness and free from suffering.

A personal anecdote will place this all in context. A few years ago, a neighbor put us to the test. As soon as the neighbor moved next door to us, he regularly came up with reasons to complain to us about one thing or another. There was always some problem or issue that he would immediately bring to our attention. A level of discord grew between us until it reached its climax one day, when he vested himself with the authority to haphazardly chop the branches of our bay trees framing the front of our home. He cemented horrible broken glass bottles on top of our dividing wall contiguous to his property and over a section of our front fence to protect himself from potential thieves on the look-out who could trespass our property and later break into his. His actions were motivated by paranoia because he believed our trees were too lush and that someone could easily hide behind them to plan an ambush and break into our respective homes. You may probably imagine the reaction of a nature lover such as myself upon seeing the mutilated branches of two beautiful bay trees, haphazardly maimed with a machete in what appeared to be a vicious and violent act of beastly defiance. My heart was bleeding.

We filed a police report for illegal trespass and property damage and advised the neighbor of the impending criminal and civil charges against him which would require him to dispense with plenty of time and money and retain very good attorneys for his defense. The battle of the egos began—the battle of "victims" against "villain."

We fixed the damages to our fence in a way that was both aesthetic and secure which, as a bonus feature, served as a privacy shield to avoid seeing the neighbor and prevent any further interactions with him. Slowly, the bay trees grew once more, recovering their shape, their branches lush with beautiful green leaves. Our heated emotions began to cool down. A period of reflection ensued—time to reflect on what had transpired and confront our unconsciousness.

These incidents revealed to me the multiple dimensions of my ego. They unveiled my level of attachment to my possessions (my house, my fence, and my trees), of my non-acceptance of events as they occurred, and my non-acceptance of my neighbor's behavior and his state of consciousness. It revealed a level of pride in my reaction to the perceived audacity and abuse of my neighbor's actions. I demonstrated wrong speech and feelings of anger and resentment. I blamed him, not only for the damages, but also for my emotions, thereby feeling justified in unleashing all the negative feelings he triggered in me.

Then one evening, I decided to seek the spiritual solution and the underlying lesson hidden in this episode. I decided to meditate in order to enter a space of inner silence and stillness, seeking insight and an opening to compassion regarding my neighbor and me. Slowly, I began to see our shared humanity with my soul and felt the oneness of our spirits at the deepest level of Self, beyond the masks of our respective egos. I saw that my neighbor, as well as me, with all of our faults and virtues, were beings who were loved and valued by someone in this lifetime—that we derived from the same creative source that engendered us into this human experience where each of us had a purpose for being. I saw that both of us, and the rest of humanity, were trying to navigate through this life's journey as best we could, trying to heal our suffering along the way. I understood that my neighbor's actions were motivated by his fear, impelled by a frantic state of insecurity, whether true or unfounded, and that my reactions were propelled by my ego or unconsciousness. All of my resentment started to slowly melt away and was soon replaced by a warm, tingling sensation in my heart.

I felt my heart expanding and radiating a palpable energy of tenderness and compassion towards my neighbor.

I changed my frequency regarding the incident by expanding my consciousness to a deep state of acceptance, understanding, and compassion for my neighbor and myself—I felt a sense of Oneness. I took responsibility for changing the only thing I could: my energy, the frequency to which I would align, my thoughts and perceptions about the unfolding circumstances and my neighbor. I changed my state of consciousness.

We may verily choose to perceive the guilty party in our drama as a villain and feel anger over a given situation. However, from a state of consciousness of acceptance, you will begin to see that you cannot control the thoughts, perceptions, and behavior of others. The act of accepting events as they are, not as we would like them to be, is the first step towards spiritual maturity which guides us to a new reality. By accepting even the most difficult of situations, you take responsibility for modifying the only thing you can transform, your perception about any unpleasant life circumstance and about the individuals involved. After assuming responsibility for your emotions and your personal state of consciousness, after meditating and mindfully contemplating the situation, you begin to raise your vibrational energy and frequency level. You begin to observe that those whom you formerly perceived as villains and authors of your suffering are most often victims themselves. Aligned to this new state of consciousness, you realize that those who cause the alleged injury do not know that they are, in fact, divine beings, that they are spiritual beings living a human experience. You actually reach an awakened and expansive state where you perceive that both parties to the drama are innocent "victims" of a false sense of power and of the nebulous fog of unconsciousness which enshrouds them obscuring their vision, and you realize that anyone sharing this inner state of sightlessness deserves compassion. When both parties are aligned with their false sense of "I" (false sense of self), both the "villain" due to the quality of his actions, and the "victim" due to the quality of her reactions, share the same illness—ego unconsciousness.

Many unconscious actions are based on fear, insecurity, attachment to possessions, fear of loss, judgment of others, pride, and false power, all of which derive from ego and from the veil that hides the greatness of our Higher Self and the expansiveness of our true essence. We all experience moments of weakness when our energy is depleted and our ego takes full advantage of these vulnerable moments. When you are aware of this, you begin to see yourself and others with eyes of compassion, because you can perceive the different levels of suffering and their destructive effects to your physical, emotional and spiritual well-being and the equally harmful impact on the welfare of all the co-participants in your life.

In this more expansive state of consciousness, you understand that there are no villains or enemies, only innocent beings lost in darkness. In this new movie, there are no villains, heroes or heroines. You cease judgment because you see your humanity and spirit reflected in those whom you once believed to have caused you, and your loved ones, injury. Aligned to this new positive frequency where love and compassion prevail, your enemies and your problems disappear, you gain a new perspective on life situations, and a new reality emerges. The object of discord stops being a problem and a reason for worry as if completely erased from your mind and consciousness.

Who changed, my neighbor and the situation, or the consciousness of that whom initially perceived him as a villain, at fault for everything that had transpired? Reality transformed itself immediately when the observer in me accepted the suchness of events as they were, when I chose the path of non-resistance regarding the circumstances I was facing and regarding my neighbor's consciousness. My reality transformed itself when the observer in me, at the level of my Higher Self, decided to take responsibility for modifying her perceptions and the energy frequency to which she aligned her awareness. By raising the energy level of my consciousness (awareness) to a more expansive spiritual state, I transformed my reality instantly. In fact, because energy is matter and carries with it information about our intentions and perceptions, this new positive energy radiated from within me and was immediately transmitted to my neighbor. Changing my energy frequency or level resulted in my neighbor's own change in energy level. We transformed our relationship and currently get along quite well—we cooperate with one another, and there is no animosity or discord between us; we are at peace. Transformation and solutions to apparent problems always initiate from within ourselves, by turning our external focus around to our inner space and wisdom, the expansive space of our Inner Master or Higher Self.

It is important to highlight that acceptance should never be confused with resignation—acceptance is not passive. Acceptance is a state of clarity in the face of change and impermanence when confronting the inevitable ups and downs of life's roller coaster. Acceptance means we stop living Life in a constant state of defensiveness; we cease resisting the course and content of our lives and our world. The state of acceptance is a prelude to responsible actions grounded on an awakened consciousness and the stability of our Higher Self.

BEYOND FORGIVENESS

Forgiveness implies judgment and guilt. Forgiveness carries the implicit judgment of "good" and "bad" actions. When we practice acceptance, non-resistance, and responsibility, we expand to a state of consciousness where forgiveness is no longer necessary; it is no longer important and serves no purpose. Instead of forgiving ourselves and others, which implies our judgment that someone behaved wrongly, we simply let go of unpleasant situations, unease, and the negative emotions triggered in us by external provocations. We let go of resentments and disturbing emotions that we may feel about ourselves, activated by undesirable stimuli engendered by those with whom we interact and by the challenging and sometimes troublesome situations we confront daily.

Rather than think in terms of forgiveness, we can instead choose to think in terms of acceptance—accepting actions, events, and the energy of those with whom we interact closely and those we view from a distance, opting to let go of any negative emotions or effects triggered in us. At this state of consciousness, we let go of the feelings and thoughts that result in our suffering through the mindful practice of non-judgment, compassion, and equanimity, becoming aware, through the deepest understanding of our Self, that no one can act or behave beyond their given state of consciousness. Rooted in a state of consciousness that extends beyond forgiveness, we see with the eyes of our soul understanding that actions which appear to cause injury to ourselves and the world are in fact grounded in the blind innocence of the parties involved. We can see with eyes of compassion and non-judgment because we know that the accountability system of the Universe leaves no debt unpaid. At this state, we are aware that karma is impersonal and that innocent perpetrators of unconscious actions simply know not what they do. These individuals are innocent because they do not realize that by aligning themselves with negative, low-frequency energy patterns, they are in fact attracting the same toxic energy into their lives. They do not know that they are accumulating a negative karmic debt with the Universe, and they are unaware that they are the cause of their suffering. When you expand your awareness to a state beyond forgiveness, you practice acceptance without judging or blaming others for their actions. When you observe the effects caused by human unconsciousness objectively, you experience a spiritual opening which results in a deep compassion for the innocence you witness in yourself, those around you, and at the collective level (your city, your nation, and the world). Rooted in this state beyond forgiveness, you finally take responsibility for letting go of negative emotions that block your spiritual growth. You begin to change the quality of your perceptions, thoughts, words, and actions thereby transforming your state of consciousness (awareness) and your quality of life.

Whenever you face an unpleasant or challenging situation, you can raise your energy and state of consciousness instantly by following these steps:

1. By accepting conditions and events, no matter how difficult or unpleasant, exactly as they are (accepting the suchness of what is);

2. By offering non-resistance regardless of the situation, no matter how difficult;
3. By not reacting defensively in the face of adversity;
4. By remaining committed to your intention and discipline of being grounded in positive energy notwithstanding the circumstances. Before acting or reacting you may ask yourself:

   - ✓ What is my intention in wanting to blame ____?
   - ✓ What do I wish to gain by blaming ___ (or by resisting this situation)? What do I believe is the payoff?
   - ✓ Do I wish to manipulate emotions, control behavior, or change the situation?
   - ✓ Am I acting from my ego, identifying myself as either the victim or hero of this drama, or am I acting from the compassionate wisdom of my Inner Master or Higher Self?

5. By taking responsibility for modifying your perceptions, thoughts, emotions and energy when confronted with a difficult situation. You may ask yourself:

   - ✓ How can I perceive or respond from an energy or space that is consistent with my Higher Self?

6. By changing your old perceptions and frequency to a positive higher energy state where an awareness grounded in nonjudgment, faith, optimism, harmony, understanding, compassion, love, and peace operate, regardless of the challenging circumstances you face.

7. By acting and reacting from the stability of your Higher Self, seeking spiritual solutions from a state of consciousness that is free from judgment and rooted in Understanding, Compassion, Love, Peace and Oneness.

Practicing this method allows us to begin unblocking the negative patterns that create the obstacles that prevent us from experiencing the richness, happiness, expansiveness and fullness of life. By practicing acceptance, non-resistance, and responsibility, we discard the old perceptions and negative emotions that block our growth in terms of health, happiness, and love, and which hinder our spiritual expansion towards Enlightenment. Awakening to this state of consciousness (awareness), we understand that the path to transformation is entirely our responsibility and no one else's. We can see with a newfound state of clarity the wisdom of St. Francis of Assisi who reminds us that it is our responsibility to selflessly give light, understanding, hope, and love rather than wait for these gifts as passive recipients.

When we adopt this new pattern before any challenging situation with discipline and mindfulness, we automatically ascend to superior energy levels that correspond to an expansive state of consciousness and where the authentic power of our Higher Self becomes evident in every one of our actions, resulting in positive karma and a fruitful harvest.

7

FROM FRAGMENTATION TO ONENESS CONSCIOUSNESS

*By expanding your frame of vision,
every fragmented piece will become
integrated into a beautiful and
harmonious panoramic view of reality.*

In the material world of forms—our relative reality in which our human experience unfolds—we become accustomed to a fragmented reality founded on comparisons, categories and distinctions, where our experience of reality is composed of broken differentiated parts and where we cannot always appreciate the integrity or wholeness connecting all the pieces. Our limited experience of the physical world involves an observation of reality that operates on the basis of differences and dualities. For example, we experience reality in terms of good/bad, light/darkness, loss/gain, good luck/bad luck, suffering/happiness, and love/hate. When we comprise our reality exclusively from physical reality, and the duality of the material world, we limit our vision of reality, of the Universe, and of ourselves. Whenever we face challenging situations that we define as bad, or when we believe to have bad luck, we connect to a fragmented consciousness where the limited vision of our reality does not encompass the deeper, absolute reality which is the Oneness or Wholeness of the Universe.

Much in the same way that we are not the labels by which we define ourselves or the labels imposed on us by the outside world, the situations we face are neither good nor bad, they simply are. At the level of Wholeness or Oneness, beyond fragmentation, there is a perfect balance where there is neither loss nor gain, good or bad. For example, at the level of fragmentation, we may perceive that winning the lottery is good luck and will result in our happiness and well-being. However, we may not recognize the possibility that it may also lead to suffering and a chain reaction of negative events. Stemming from a level of Wholeness, it is understood that an apparent "good" may give rise to something "bad" and that a "negative" event may, in fact, lead to something "positive." When we surrender the labels imposed by our fragmented material world, we surrender ourselves defenselessly before a Divine Intelligence that moves the entire Universe. We open ourselves to all possibilities placed before us with faith and trust that the Universe operates with synchronistic precision and perfect order within apparent chaos. In fact, that which appears to be chaos is nothing more than a product of our limited consciousness conditioned by a fragmented reality within the world of dualities. As long as our consciousness remains limited by a fragmented view of reality, we will not experience the abundance, perfection and Wholeness of the Universe in our personal lives.

For example, if you experience difficulties at work, excessive stress levels, humiliation from your boss or co-workers, or any level of personal dissatisfaction, you may choose to view your experience from a limited state of awareness, complaining about your bad luck and level of discontent, and remain mired in your suffering, fearing the loss of the apparent financial stability offered by your employment and salary. However, you may also choose to view this as a transitory situation that perhaps provides the opportunity to liberate yourself from your suffering altogether, by changing employments or propelling you to change careers. You may also consider starting your own company with the opportunity of greater independence, the potential for higher revenues or even more free time. From this supposed "negative" situation you may potentially expand to new and exciting horizons that perhaps you may not have otherwise considered.

The same can occur with an apparently beneficial situation. For example, there are plenty of documentaries showcasing the lives of lottery winners where "good luck" has turned sour, often resulting in the envy and hostility of friends, family, and neighbors. In other cases, excessive consumerism and economic instability take over the winners stemming from the erroneous belief that their fortunes would last them a lifetime. I have also seen many cases where winners end up losing their entire fortunes.

When we learn to accept situations as they unfold before us, without adding any qualifiers, without judging them as good or bad, we take responsibility for our reactions at life's every turn, because we acquire a more expansive view of life. With this new vision, we understand that in reality there is no loss or gain. We can appreciate the movement of the contents of life like waves that initiate, reach their apex and then subside as they descend to eventually rise once more. We reach this level of acceptance when we understand that reality extends far beyond the labels and the world of duality that we observe with our senses. Our material experience of the world will present us with ups and downs because nothing in the material world is permanent. By accepting the impermanence of our material world, we also learn to practice detachment. Assimilating the truth of impermanence and change, we become aware that most of our suffering is a result of attachment to material things, situations or individuals, none of which are permanent. We know all this in theory, but in practice we live with the characteristic innocence of our human unconsciousness both at the individual and collective levels.

Nature reveals to us the cycles of perpetual movement, impermanence and transformation, all of which are part of a fragmented reality. The sun and the moon have their cycles as well as the seasons: winter, spring, summer and fall. We observe the cycles of a tree whose leaves fall in autumn, leaving behind bare branches which will once again burst with blooms of spring promise. We see that a beautiful rose withers and fades, its organic matter disintegrates with a putrid odor, which later serves as compost for new rose bushes and crops, delivering beautifully fragrant blossoms and nourishment to our body, mind, and soul. When we are able to accept and see the reality of these cycles without attachment, we cease to suffer, trusting that each cycle comes to its inevitable end to initiate and give rise to a new process. We see beyond the scope of relative reality, within the limited world of forms, to encompass a view of absolute reality. Our vision expands from a state of fragmented consciousness to one of Wholeness or Oneness.

When we expand towards a consciousness of Wholeness, we experience the wisdom of the Universe's balance at a very personal level. If we observe closely, we will perceive that when something "bad" or "unpleasant" happens, we often become depressed, disheartened and absorbed in a cycle of negative thoughts, fixing our attention pointedly on our affliction. Sometimes, we become submerged in our suffering, believing there is no escape and that our personal world has crumbled completely. However, if at such moments we were to take inventory of all the "good" or "pleasant" situations we have had the privilege of experiencing, we would soon realize that there are probably plenty of these as well. By taking inventory of every situation we have experienced, we will likely come to the realization that there is a balance between the pleasant and not so pleasant moments of our lives. Therefore, when we confront challenging moments, which we all undoubtedly do, let us remind ourselves that we have also lived moments of pleasure and happiness. We must gently remind ourselves that difficult moments are simply situations, they are simply one more content of our lives but in no way do they define our lives, and are not Life itself. Disquieting moments offer us invaluable opportunities to recognize what, in fact, provokes or triggers our afflictions, so as to learn from them, to grow and perhaps even to show others how to navigate the turbulent waters of their own difficult storms.

In the world of duality, nothing is permanent, which means that even our most daunting moments will also reach their inevitable end. We must remind ourselves when facing these overwhelming moments that these too shall pass. When we accept this reality, we transcend to a point beyond a consciousness of fragmentation replacing it instead with a state of Oneness Consciousness. Rooted in this new expansive state of Wholeness or Oneness, we maintain a state of centeredness appreciating that, in our material existence, we cannot experience moments of happiness without also having lived bitter moments of sorrow and pain. We cannot experience light without the presence of darkness, nor can we experience the relief of peace without having experienced moments of anguish and unease. We cannot fully appreciate the miraculous gift of life in our material human incarnation without recognizing and accepting the impermanence of this experience and our eventual and inevitable material disintegration. Transcendence to an enlightened consciousness would also be impossible without the blind darkness of unconsciousness.

The Chinese symbol of Yin-Yang is the perfect graphic example of Fragmentation and Oneness. The Chinese tradition recognizes that when a situation develops to its extreme expression, it undoubtedly reaches its point of return, transforming itself into its opposite expression. Reality is recognized as wholeness, oneness, or the totality which is known as Tao. Tao is the natural order of the Universe. The graphic symbol of Yin-Yang is symmetrical but not static. It symbolizes a rotating force of a continuous cyclical movement. Divided into light and darkness, it represents opposite poles and each pole already contains within itself the seed of its opposite expression. This flux means that the natural flow of Yin/Yang operates in such a way that, when either force reaches its maximum expression, the cycle ends, thus initiating the expression of the opposite force. This cycle continues to rotate in perpetuity within the relative reality of our physical world of material formations, the world of fragmented reality. To limit our vision to just one pole is to not accept the natural movement of the Universe, it is similar to limiting ourselves to a dark prison where our sense of reality is only a shadow of the truth which causes great suffering. To understand the Tao is to expand our consciousness to a reality of Wholeness or Totality. In this state of consciousness, we can see the truth—we can touch deep reality and flow with the natural and harmonious rhythm of Divine Cosmic Intelligence.

When we accept the impermanence of our experiences and of this physical world in which we live, we learn to accept that pleasurable moments are also transitory. Recognition and acceptance of impermanence do not mean that pleasurable and joyful moments lose their value or that we must suffer by acknowledging their impermanence. On the contrary, to awaken to the deep reality of Universal Oneness allows us to savor, with maximum enthusiasm, surrender, and presence, the uniqueness of each magical moment we experience in this lifetime. When we transcend from a fragmented vision to a consciousness of Oneness, we are able to maintain a healthy balance that allows us to observe all of our personal experiences and the situations in our environment grounded in tranquility and equanimity. This results in a depth of vision or spiritual insight that influences every other aspect of our lives in a holistic manner which includes our body, mind and spirit, our personal and business relationships, and our social and political perspectives. It allows us to see the nature of the material world objectively accepting that, within the fragmented world of duality, everything that increases must eventually subside and all that descends will once again rise. Accepting this phenomenon, we can observe the different cycles and stages that unfold in our lives, at the personal and collective levels, without judgment or attachment, understanding that change is the natural movement of life and that perpetual transformation is an integral part of the human experience.

As soon as we are able to accept the fragmentation of the physical world, we experience the changing phases of life with detachment, and we expand to a state of consciousness of Oneness, beyond fragmentation, where we open ourselves to a fuller human existence characterized by a greater state of aliveness and intensity within each moment. At this new state of awareness, we understand that we must not take any experience for granted, but at the same time, we realize that we must also not identify with any one experience completely, because every one of our experiences is impermanent. We are able to live more deeply and mindfully, contemplating each moment of joy as well as our loved ones with greater attention, presence, gratitude, devotion and surrender, knowing that each of our loved ones and every joyful moment is ephemeral and therefore an invaluable treasure.

When we awaken to this reality and accept it fully and responsibly, we can walk freely in the world of duality fearlessly and non-defensively in what we once considered a cruel and unjust world characterized by random capriciousness. The act of awakening to the absolute reality of Oneness that extends beyond the fragmented physical world, is freedom from suffering and from the prison of limited vision where we perceive only one dimension of the Truth. Our consciousness awakens to the absolute reality that suffering and happiness are not in fact "two" but part of one Whole. In this expansive state, we touch our true essence; we are more authentically who we are—awakened observers aligned to the totality of an integrated universal consciousness which is the source of Infinite Divine Intelligence, of Truth, and Oneness.

Aligned to a state of consciousness of Oneness (Wholeness or Totality), we reconnect with a profound and absolute state of true Peace and Happiness; a state of consciousness which is permanent. It is reconnecting with our true essence at the spiritual level, a state of Oneness or Universal Wholeness/Totality that is in fact permanent and infinite. When we operate from this expansive state, we remain centered in the quiet wisdom of our Higher Self, characterized by a balanced stability, a state of equanimity, calmness, trust and surrender even under the most volatile of turbulences that shake us along this brief journey through this lifetime. At the same time, we live our most beautiful moments, no matter how small, with the same joyful delight and impetuous intensity of a young lover eternally in love with Life.

Aligned with this state of consciousness of Wholeness, we receive every moment life presents to us in the world of duality with detachment and non-identification. We live each experience without feeling either attachment or aversion to any. Realizing that nothing is either permanent or belongs to us in this lifetime, we enjoy the pleasure of the physical world without attachment but with eternal gratitude for the precious gift offered us each instant to delight in them. We reach a state where nothing that happens matters to us because we realize that no situation belongs to us or defines us, regardless of how unpleasant or how pleasurable it may be. Whatever transpires slowly becomes less significant and our reactions to whatever occurs begin to take center stage—our new priority becomes choosing acceptance and inner peace over suffering. We travel through life with the tranquility and emotional equilibrium of the sages, and we smile onto life with the wise half-smile of the Enlightened.

THE LAKE AND HER WATER-LILLIES

The neighbors at the lake complained that the lake's aquatic vegetation (water-lilies) was increasing in number and density with each passing summer. They said the lake would turn into a swamp if we did not take immediate action to resolve this problem. The aquatic plants were growing within a small area and bordered some sections of the lake's outer edges, but what the neighbors perceived as weeds or a problem was nature's perfect expression. Each element in nature has a function and exhibits perfect order. The leaves which fall each autumn from the surrounding trees have been nourishing the lake annually. The earth's tendency is to reclaim its terrain while, at the same time, generating life. Nature's impulse is the reason water-lilies grow around the lake's edge, taking root wherever the lake is shallowest. At the same time, the water-lilies provide the lake with ample shade, keeping it cool in the summer to prevent the production of toxic bacteria and algae that are harmful to humans and animals. Water-lilies attract insects and these rest on their green leaves and white blooms where frogs and birds approach for their feedings, always finding an abundance of nourishment. The lake and its surroundings are an active ecosystem of flora and fauna, the perfect example of giving and receiving in full function. Everything reflects a perfect order within the apparent chaos.

When I navigate to the center of the lake, there is no aquatic vegetation on its surface because the center is the lake's deepest point. From the lake's serene center, taking in the entire panoramic view of the surroundings, one cannot distinguish the aquatic vegetation that is such a nuisance and eyesore at the edge of the dock and from each neighbor's lakeshore. Instead, one sees subtle waves where flashes of glittering sun bounce happily off the lake's surface. The perfect balance of beautiful water-lilies contributes an aura of magical splendor to the lake, and the pines and leafy trees reflect in the luminous mirror of the lake's surface. One can hear the birds and frogs sing, and occasionally, the sudden sound of fish, playfully leaping from the lake. There is no swampy, aquatic overgrowth or chaos at the center of the lake, there is only serenity, beauty and harmony. From its center, one absorbs the totality of the lake and its environment, wise in its apparent disorder, beautiful and perfect in its imperfection. Each element of the surrounding environment contributes an artistic tone to the canvas and an impeccable chord to the musical harmony of this enchanting place. It is a true inexhaustible exposition of Unconditional Love (*See a photo of Lake Claire and water-lilies on back cover*).

If we limit ourselves to simply observing and navigating the outermost edge of the lake, we will continuously become tangled and stuck on the lake's surface overgrowth and dense underwater roots, causing us aggravation and suffering. From that limited perspective, reality is comprised of merely the lake's surface and the vegetation's unpleasant nuisance, the full panoramic view escapes us, and we cannot truly enjoy the lake. However, by navigating far beyond the lake's shallow edge, we are able to paddle effortlessly to the deeper center of the lake where we may now observe from a distance and with detachment. We gain a newly expanded scope of vision where we can now see what we were previously unable to fully appreciate from a limited vantage point or perspective. We transform our reality completely, bringing our initial state of suffering to an end.

The same holds true in life where we must amplify our frame of vision to encompass the whole panoramic view. In this way, we will appreciate that everything has its implicit order and beauty when we choose to see with the eyes of our soul, from a state of consciousness of Oneness, Wholeness or Totality. Detaching from the incessant need to have the perfect view from our personal shore (ego/fragmented consciousness) we are able to see with equanimity, fully enjoying the perfection of the entire lake and its surrounding environment as a Whole. From this state of consciousness of Wholeness or Oneness, we extend our dock to the deep waters at the center of our lake and, from the depth of this quiet center, we blissfully navigate the serene waters of our own spirit or True Self.

8

THE PRESENT IS A GIFT

"If you are depressed, you are living in
the past. If you are anxious, you are living
in the future. If you are at peace, you
are living in the present." ~ Lao Tzu

The present is the only absolute or eternal dimension
that exists. The entire content of our lives takes shape
within the timelessness of the present. Everything unfolds
Now. Today is one eternal day. The dimensions of past and
future are concepts that only exist in our minds; they are
concepts of our imagination. When we travel back to the
past or into the future, we do so with our thoughts, and
each time we do so, it is always now, in the present.

Liberation from the prison of the past and the future
is available in the present when we practice acceptance
and mindfulness in order to maintain a state of conscious
presence. This distinction is important because we may often
resist the content of our present which results in suffering.
To truly find inner peace and freedom from affliction in the
Now, it is important to practice acceptance and mindfulness.

MINDFULNESS AND PRESENCE

The practice of present moment awareness or mindfulness liberates us from the ghosts of the past and tormentors of the future which constantly invade our minds and which provoke suffering and anxiety of that which once was and no longer is, and that which has yet to be. Now is the only true dimension that exists and every moment we have lived has taken place in the present.

When you travel with your mind to the past or the future, you deny yourself the gift of the present. To evade the present is to sleepwalk through life where each precious moment of what is NOW passes you by without actually living it entirely or deeply; your body ambles through life like a robot, with your mind in a haze-like state of daydreaming, conditioned by your past. Your turn to live this worldly experience is impermanent, therefore, when you resist the present moment you are rejecting the most precious gift that has been offered you. It is the equivalent of denying Life itself.

I know an individual who is enduring a chronic coronary illness and after several medical interventions is currently waiting for a heart transplant. This person explained to me that prior to his diagnosis, he lived a frenzied, agitated life, constantly worrying about each difficulty he encountered. He often felt impatient and frustrated when he was asked to wait and he worked excessively. After his medical diagnosis, everything changed. He awakened to a new state of consciousness where he sees each present moment as a gift. He now recognizes that what once disturbed him no longer does. He understands that the present is a prized treasure and, acknowledging it as the only moment that exists, he now lives each moment deeply, fully and joyfully. Now he marvels at the moments of impatience and frustration he once experienced before his diagnosis, moments in which he wasted the present by stressing and agonizing over situations not worth suffering over. Now he faces life in a state of calm and lives each moment bestowed on him with happiness. He smiles to himself whenever he observes the frenzied movement of people about the city, the anxiety and frustration of drivers in bumper to bumper traffic at evening rush hour, the constant obsession with work and money, and the incessant complaints about insignificant things within the grand scheme of life. This individual fully accepts that his existence is not guaranteed, yet, he does not complain about his illness, does not consider himself a victim and has no fear. He emanates great optimism, a highly positive energy and inner peace which is absolutely inspiring.

It is quite common for people facing hardships due to chronic illness, or who are suddenly confronting their mortality, to awaken to a state of consciousness where the present moment takes on a newfound priority and sense of aliveness. Under such circumstances, one lives each moment as it if were simultaneously the first and last. Some individuals seek to experience the depth of the present moment, either consciously or unconsciously, through high-risk activities such as skydiving or speed racing, among others. These and other high-risk activities require an increased pointed concentration in the present moment where any slight lapse in attention may result in an accident or even death. In such a state, one lives a more vibrant dimension of the present which in turn adds an intensity that cannot be replicated under run-of-the-mill, daily activities. These sensations are not just the product of an adrenaline rush, but the effects of increased vitality that results from the act of completely surrendering to the present without anything else invading our mental space, thus creating an opening into the dimension of Being that transcends thoughts and ego. Others may instead seek moments that require complete surrender and devoted, detailed attention such as in painting, playing an instrument or fishing at a serene lake, to name a few. Now, we must not only seek certain activities that imbue us with a sense of deep presence or wait until a stressful ordeal, such as a serious illness or suddenly facing our imminent mortality, to immerse ourselves in this eternal dimension. We can surrender and live the present moment deeply and fully in this very moment with each breath...now.

It is quite easy to let yourself be carried away by the strong current of thoughts, worries and challenging circumstances rushing through our minds and lives. Perhaps many consider the task would, in fact, be easier outside of the daily grind encountered at work, with bills and obligations, instead sitting by the beach on a deserted island or in the tranquil environment of the mountains. I understand it perfectly. While working on this book, I encountered simultaneous imposing circumstances: my imminent move to a new office, a slew of pending cases and a caseload of new clients as I worked on transitioning to my new office, I still needed to contract someone to make repairs at my new commercial space, I needed to coordinate the utility transfer to avoid work interruption, suddenly I received a personal call requiring my immediate attention abroad, I received persistent calls from an out-of-state client requesting my assistance prior to closing on his new home, I still needed to arrange some repairs pending at my home, in other words, the list was never ending, and I still needed to finish this book.

Whenever I felt the onset of anxiety, I concentrated on my breathing and let go of the emotions and thoughts triggering my discomfort. I made my mind still through silence and meditation and only worked on whatever proceeded at the moment, fully surrendered to the present without thinking about tomorrow or the next day, just undertaking the task at hand. I trusted that everything would unfold perfectly, staying centered within my quiet inner space, mindfully contemplating the present moment.

It is impossible to do everything at once. Sometimes, we believe ourselves more productive when we multitask, but when we try to tend to everything at once, we trigger unnecessary anxiety in ourselves and are only half-way efficient in our production levels. Realistically, you can only complete one thing at a time and at the precise moment in which it is required. For example, if you cannot sleep on a Saturday at 2AM thinking about a work issue that needs to be resolved, there is nothing you can do at that precise moment until you return to your office on Monday morning. The act of thinking, or rather, worrying about that which cannot be resolved at a given moment is a common mechanism by which we escape the present moment.

To relieve yourself of stress and anxiety, you can practice returning to mindful presence any time your mind escapes to the past or future, or whenever a strong emotion takes over, pulling you out of accepting the unfolding of present circumstances. Anytime you are invaded by an avalanche of thoughts and situations that distract you from now, stop, breathe, and mindfully contemplate the present moment. Simply by stopping, breathing, and recognizing that you are not present, you will return to the state of mindful, present moment awareness.

You can cultivate presence daily with each daily task, with your housework, job responsibilities, daily conversations and interactions, and as you shop for groceries. For example, this means that while you are having dinner, you become mindful of what you consume and bring your entire conscious awareness to those with whom you are sharing that moment, you do not let your mind trail off to what you will do tomorrow or what TV program you will watch after dinner. If you are washing your dishes, you equally surrender fully to that moment with the conscious intention that it is the sole task and your most important undertaking at the moment. You wash the dishes carefully, without rushing to finish to start another activity, you feel the sensation of the water and soap running through your fingers and notice the smooth texture of each dish. When you are at work, you carry out each responsibility with mindful presence, without anticipating your lunch hour or the end of your work day.

Whenever you bring your full awareness and presence to that which you do, you are giving your Self completely and sharing the gift of your energy, the most integral part of your Being, to whatever you devote your time and your actions. When you dedicate your time and energy with mindful presence to that which you love, time dissipates effortlessly by entering the timeless dimension of the present. When you offer your presence to your loved ones, your clients, and your life's co-participants, you are communicating in the language of your Higher Self. You connect at the most intimate and at the same time expansive state of that which unites us all as one at the spiritual and universal level. At this state of presence, you recognize yourself in others and others in yourself. By awakening to this state of consciousness, you delight in each moment where everything now feels and gains a greater sense of aliveness because you surrender your full attention to the present and to those with whom who share each moment. You are grateful for each moment's experience no matter how apparently simple it appears to be. Living fully from a state of conscious awareness in the present moment offers a unique experience of life where you connect to the deep ocean of your soul which in turn reflects the expansive ocean of the Universe.

PRESENCE AND THE HIGHER SELF

By combining mindful presence with silence and stillness, you are able to realign with your Higher Self and the source of Divine Intelligence. This combination is the formula to return home, to the internal refuge where you find peace, happiness, and freedom—freedom from the fetters of the past and preoccupation with the future. By discovering presence in your Higher Self, you liberate yourself from the shadows of the past, such as remorse and resentments which trap you in a negative cycle, and you release yourself from anxiety over your uncertainty about the future as well as from any resistance to the present. With the help of mindfulness to maintain your presence, you become the observer beyond ego. In this state of presence, you embrace each situation that unfolds in your life with acceptance, non-resistance, and responsibility in the present. To offer resistance against the content of the present moment is to fight against what is and to stand in opposition to the entire Universe.

It is from a state of presence that you enter the space of awakened consciousness that is your true essence or Higher Self. From that space, you gain access to the source of creativity, of all possibilities and of the same universal abundance that resides within you and each one of us, and which unites us all as one. In fact, quantum physics describes that we are a hologram of the universe, as concluded by the enlightening experiments of David Bohm. A hologram is a three dimensional optical image whose effect is created with a photographic plate and the application of a light treatment on different planes. The use of holograms is commonly seen in events where images of deceased celebrities are recreated and once again brought to life on stage. In a hologram, each part of the image contains the totality of the image. The holographic paradigm described by Bohm describes that everything in the universe is connected with everything else, including our human minds.[4] The scientific investigations on the topic of consciousness are increasing, and numerous scientific experiments reveal, through highly sophisticated mathematical analysis, that our brains can detect frequency patterns in other dimensions and beyond the space-time continuum. What this means is that we are co-creators of a reality that depends on the angle of our perspective and that, as such, we can reflect the same order of a much deeper reality in our own world, a reality that is beyond our limited and fragmented vision of reality.[5] As a result, this indicates that, just like a hologram, the individual mind has the capability of reflecting the entire universe, if we align ourselves with a consciousness of Integrity or Wholeness which is a reality that offers us an existence of Totality or Oneness with the whole Universe.[6]

Once more we see that the conclusions and studies of quantum physics complement a deep and absolute reality of Oneness described by mystics and which we previously delved into on the topic of fragmentation and expansion to a consciousness of Wholeness or Totality. The holographic paradigm of David Bohm also reflects the field of infinite abundance, of Divine Intelligence which is the source of creation from which we all derive. If our individual mind has the capacity to reflect the entire universe, this perfectly explains the mechanism by which, connected to the frequency of the field of Oneness, we can manifest all of our desires with the power of intention. By aligning ourselves with this infinite field, we are accessing the abundance of the Universe, and reflecting it in our own lives at the individual level.

Only through mindful, present moment awareness are we able to access the field of all possibilities and Pure Consciousness (Infinite Consciousness). By maintaining a conscious, awakened presence, we assume responsibility for aligning ourselves with the authentic power of our spirit rather than with the false power of our ego. The heart of our authentic power is our Higher Self, Divine Source, or God, our true essence which resides within us. When we reconnect with our Inner Master/Teacher, our authentic power manifests itself through our every action in what is, in fact, our spiritual movement within this material world. At the level of our authentic power or Higher Self, we live a conscious humanity, making awakened decisions that are grounded on our most enlightened consciousness which includes a state of deep understanding, compassion, love, and peace. The opposite of authentic power is force. Force, which is ego's false sense of power, takes place in the impermanent material world. Shackled by our ego, we fall prisoners to suffering and human unconsciousness, a state of unconsciousness where actions are based on satisfying the insatiable desires of our ego. Human unconsciousness is a state of innocence that ignores both the infinite expansiveness and wisdom of our Being as well as the key to true Freedom.

It is from this very state of presence that we practice acceptance, non-resistance and responsibility, as discussed previously. It is also from this state of mindful, awakened presence that we are able to enter the state beyond forgiveness where we detach from negative emotions, thoughts, and patterns as a result of past conditioning and which create obstacles to our spiritual growth, material progress, and a superior quality of life.

PRESENT MOMENT AWARENESS: EGO'S ENEMY

Ego exists within the horizontal dimension of time that pertains to relative reality and the material world as experienced by our senses. This horizontal dimension is where past and future exist; it is the world in which we have created the division of time to facilitate our movement and development in the physical world. It is the distribution of time into minutes, hours, days, months, years; it is the perception of time on your clock and calendar where the illusion of yesterday and today exist as real.

The Higher Self, Pure Consciousness, Infinite Field of Possibilities, or spirit, resides in the vertical dimension that we can only access in the present and which is timeless. The present is the only dimension in which you can experiment the true essence of Being. It is the only dimension that has been and will always be because it is infinite and eternal.

The ego is an enemy of the present. The ego resists the present because, once we awaken to the timelessness of Now, ego is powerless and ceases to exist. Ego can only exist, nourish and strengthen itself from our attachments to the impermanent material world where time and physical space exist. The ego sustains itself through constant dissatisfaction, by complaining and by resisting the conditions and contents of the present moment.

The present moment is the dimension where you can readily access the internal space that is your true essence, the awakened consciousness of your Higher Self that has always been and will always be. There resides the silent observer that observes ego and all that takes place in the physical world without judgment. Firmly centered in the present with an awakened awareness, your ego loses its strength and begins to disintegrate.

We may compare both horizontal and vertical dimensions with the ocean. The ocean's surface is the horizontal dimension where the ego emerges and expands. The surface of the ocean is in constant flux, with high and low tides in the space of one given day and waves that change according to the time and season. The ocean's surface is a perfect metaphor for the material world and the horizontal movement of our human experience where time, yesterday and tomorrow, past and future exist.

The depth of the ocean can be compared to the vertical dimension where spirit and the Higher Self resides. Deep within the sea, there is tranquility and silence, a space where one is unable to perceive even the most tumultuous of waves or anything else that takes place on the surface.

Our human experience is comprised of both dimensions. If we navigate life merely on the surface, unaware of the ocean's hidden depth, we would be limiting ourselves to living and experiencing only one dimension of reality. We would spend our entire lives tumbled about by the strong ocean waves, like a ship adrift in a storm, about to capsize into the sea. Waiting for the storm to subside, we would be anxiously anticipating our enjoyment of calmer waters ahead, or perhaps wishing to return to old ports of call visited once upon a time along our long voyage. Perhaps we would also feel anguish and remorse for not having taken an alternate course to avoid the storm altogether. Nonetheless, it is possible to experience the surface as well as the inner depth of life's majestic ocean. By expanding towards a consciousness that encompasses both the surface and the inner depth of the sea, we would be sure to find inner calm even when confronted by life's strongest tempests; we would find our return home to our Inner Master, our Higher Self...Now.

OCEAN

EGO

Past ---------------- Surface ------------ *Future*

Present
HIGHER SELF
Depth

Some call the depth of this awakened, silent space the Inner Christ or Christ Consciousness and others call it the state of Buddha Consciousness. The term Buddha does not describe a person but a state of enlightened consciousness. In Sanskrit, Buddha describes a state of mental tranquility, a spiritual state of awakened illumination or enlightenment. Siddhartha Gautama (490/450-410/370 BCE) transcended to a state of spiritual enlightenment and is therefore known as the Buddha or The Enlightened One. In his "Map of Consciousness," Dr. Hawkins measures the calibration of the Christ and Buddha state at 1000, which is the state of consciousness of highest energy frequency calibration measured in our human experience thus far.[7]

In this awakened state of mindful presence nothing is missing, you are complete—you are whole. In that space, everything is revealed to you and illuminated like never before; it is a state in which we feel connected to everything else. The formula to experience this integral state of consciousness is presence, silence, and stillness. In the Sutra (teaching), "Knowing the Better Way to Live Alone," the Buddha describes not solitude or separation from others but instead refers to liberating ourselves from the ghosts of our past and from our anticipated future, both of which inhabit and haunt our minds. The Sutra refers to living alone with the awakened clarity that comes from presence, from our deep observation of the present moment and from an inner state of calm where one experiences no desire or attachment to past or future.[8]

I personally experienced such a moment of clarity or Satori, which in Sanskrit means a sudden flash of illumination. I was observing nature deeply in the backyard of my parents' home in the Dominican Republic, without adding any description or qualitative words to what I observed, I was simply surrendered, living the suchness of the present moment fully. Everything looked and felt more alive than ever—the movement of the leaves on the mango tree, the subtle caress of the warm breeze on my skin, the colorful flutter of butterflies. I felt grateful for the serenity and deep repose available in my favorite reflective space. I take the Buddha's sutra and, reading his words, I have the illuminating revelation that at that given moment I have absolutely no desire and yet I feel whole. Everything I needed at that moment was there with me, here...Now! I was in a state of alert presence, an awakened consciousness never before felt by me until that very instant. I felt joy in the moment and complete in my aloneness. The Buddha, with his teaching of over 2000 years ago, was sharing an intimate conversation with me, describing my current and recently discovered state of repose, inner peace, and aliveness. I felt completely unattached to past or future. This moment alone existed. That moment was my first glimmer of Freedom...I smiled.

SEEING YOUR REFLECTION IN EVERYTHING

When you penetrate to an intense state of mindful presence through deep observation, you feel the aliveness of your True Self or Pure Consciousness. At the same time that you penetrate and touch the spaciousness of your true inner essence, you begin to see your Self reflected in everything. In this newfound state, you see and palpably feel an intimate and at the same time an expansive connection between yourself and the Totality.

It is a feeling that you can only know by personally living the experience. This experience is possible when you connect intimately with the Universe, becoming one with what is more expansive than yourself. This engagement is comparable to the relationship between a lover and his beloved where one merges into the other becoming One body. It is like the deep blue sea and the infinite sky which unite at the horizon, blurring the lines where one is born, and the other expires. It is a relationship analogous to a circle where there is no beginning or end between one and the other.

You can cultivate this experience through deep observation of nature's beauty. In chapter two, we discussed communing with nature as a tool to penetrate into silence, calm the mind and reconnect with our true essence. On this occasion, I am revisiting what was briefly mentioned at the end of the chapter, but prescribe yet a deeper communion with nature, one which unveils your intimate connection with something infinite and perfect—the Oneness or Divine Symphony of the Universe.

A STARRY NIGHT

Throughout my personal inner journey, experiences of deep communion with nature and an intimate relationship with the Wholeness of life have been multiplying and intensifying. I will, however, never forget the first time I had this awe-inspiring experience. I was in Nicaragua on a little known island on Lake Cocibolca. At nightfall, I stepped out with my father to enjoy the nocturnal breeze and silent night. It was an incredibly dark night, and because the island was quite distant from the mainland's coastal town of Granada, no lights could be appreciated beyond the small island.

I looked up at the jet black sky bursting with full, round, voluptuous stars; they were luminous orbs with dazzling halos. It reminded me of Van Gogh's Starry Night (1889) where the evening darkness and small town's stillness stand in sharp contrast to the brilliant, undulating movement of the night sky.[9] Until then, I had never fully captured the significant vividness of the painting. My father and I were awe-stricken; we had never before seen a starlit night quite like it.

I was completely spellbound. Looking up at the evening sky, I was overwhelmed by my infinitesimal smallness. I felt so small in comparison to the vastness of the dynamic aliveness of the cosmos, and yet, simultaneously, I felt absolutely majestic knowing that I too was a part of that amazing universe. I was stunned by my newfound sensibility which I had never before experienced— of recognizing my place within the Totality, of feeling grateful to Be and for experiencing that beautiful moment of revelation. Sharing that awe-inspiring moment with my father, I felt fortunate and humbled by our connection with the entire universe. The connection was so palpable, striking and profoundly moving that my eyes glistened with gratitude and joy.

CONNECTION WITH THE TOTALITY AND DHARMA

Once you perceive your connection to the Totality, you can feel that the Universe communicates and thinks through you. Open to this new state of awareness, you begin to transform your reality, once again complementing the holographic paradigm described by David Bohm. At this level of awareness, you recognize that you are a conduit for the universe to manifest the field of Wholeness or Oneness in your own material world. When you expand your consciousness to this state, you can clearly see the importance of aligning yourself with the divine source and the importance of making conscious choices that liberate you from ego driven decisions and from negative karma.

Once you connect with the Totality, or state of Wholeness, fully participating in an intimate relationship with Divine or Universal Intelligence (God), you begin to execute actions that are aligned with your Dharma or life's purpose. This means that, within this state, you align your actions with your Higher Self where your decisions and desires are one with the Universe—your will is one with the will of the Universe. You communicate with the Universe, you surrender to the Divine Intelligence of the Universe and the Universe responds. At this level, your guide is your spirit—your Higher Self, Divine Intelligence, Pure Consciousness, or God.

BREATHING, MINDFULNESS, AND THE PRESENT MOMENT

The best tool to access the gift of the present moment and maintain a state of mindfulness is your breath. By concentrating on your breathing, it is almost impossible to distract yourself from the present and from a state of mindfulness or awakened presence. We can use the breath like a mantra. A mantra, in Sanskrit, refers to an instrument that guides us to the space of pure consciousness beyond our thoughts and mind. You can find relief through your breath and unite body, mind, and spirit. Once you find the silent space between each inhalation and exhalation, you become centered in your true Self, centered in Being. This state is the ever-present background state of pure consciousness, the infinite state of Being which exists beyond the illusory labels of your false self or ego. By accessing this state, you liberate yourself from all tension, you detach from yesterday and tomorrow and awaken to the invaluable moment of the present.

EXERCISE

BREATHING AND MINDFULNESS: PRESENT MOMENT CONTEMPLATION

Our breath is the best instrument to center us, bring us stillness and guide us to mindfulness or conscious contemplation. This exercise uses breathing as a means to penetrate the deep ocean of the present where your true essence resides.

Sit comfortably in a silent space. Close your eyes and breathe naturally from your nose without altering the length or depth of your breathing. Place your hands on your thighs, palms facing upward. Relax your body, liberating any tension. Observe your breath as it comes in and out of your body. Observe the sound of your breath as you inhale and exhale. Notice that as you continue breathing and relaxing your body, each breath becomes deeper and your body relaxes even more. When thoughts start to invade your mind, do not judge them, let them dissipate and return to observing your breathing. Notice that the more you concentrate on your breathing, the space between each inhalation and exhalation expands. The more you observe your breathing, the more your body and mind become still. You will notice that your body and mind will feel lighter. You will feel the relief of deep inner peace. You may even notice the aliveness of certain parts of your body, like a tingling or warmth in your chest or on your hands, or perhaps throughout your entire body.

You can start practicing this exercise for 10 minutes daily and increase your practice over time. This will help you become centered within your inner space while connecting with the state of Pure Consciousness, or Field of Totality that unites us all as One. Penetrating the quiet stillness between each inhalation and exhalation, and observing the gap between each thought, you will recognize the ever-present backdrop of your pure consciousness which is your true essence and the reflection of your origin. Through the object (you) you recognize the subject (Divine Consciousness/God); the intimate connection between the lover and his beloved is unveiled before your eyes offering true vision.

You are completely present as you witness this internal space of peace and tranquility, free from any bindings to the past and the future. In your daily tasks, you will know how to reconnect to this inner space often, where your True Self resides. Anytime you observe yourself escaping or evading the present moment, concentrate on your breathing and return to the only moment that exists, Now, and reconnect with the internal wisdom of your Inner Master who will guide your actions and your purpose, aligning them in perfect harmony with the Divine Symphony.

IF NOT NOW, WHEN?

The Present offers an infinity of countless beginnings. It confers the precious gift of personal rebirth in every instant, granting the opportunity to choose at each moment as if for the first time. Today is but one day. It is therefore never too early or ever too late to make amends, to awaken, to let go of useless emotions, and to cultivate mindful intentions that contribute to evolutionary transformation. The present is a gift; it is the portal to the deep ocean of your Being where, like the deep blue mirror of the ocean reflects the sky, the light of Infinite Wholeness mirrors the inner refuge of your True Self.

If not Now, when? Now is all there is, where today is but one eternal day.

9

SECRETS OF ATTRACTION, HAPPINESS, AND ABUNDANCE

"Gratitude bestows reverence, allowing us
to encounter everyday epiphanies, those
transcendent moments of awe that change
forever how we experience life and the world."
~ John Milton (British poet 1608-1674)

ATTRACTION AND THE RIGHT OF CONSCIOUSNESS

It is important to reiterate that, with respect to energy and the natural flow of the universe, we attract what we are. We attract whatever shares the same frequency in which we vibrate and operate in life. We can therefore never expect to attract or receive more than what we offer or confer on the Universe. What you draw to yourself in the material world depends on your state of consciousness and the frequency to which you align yourself. This principle of attraction describes the mechanism by which something is rightfully yours, also referred to as, Right of Consciousness.

When you align yourself to the high energy frequency of Pure, Infinite Consciousness (your Higher Self), you attract people and situations that are attuned to your same frequency. Everything flows effortlessly because you tune-in to Divine Intelligence which places into circulation everything that you need for your evolution with perfect order and synchrony. The Universe is always in favor of your evolutionary progress. When your actions and energy align to this inherent evolutionary impulse of your spirit, you communicate your intentions and desires in an intimate conversation with the Universe, and the Universe responds. As long as you are vibrating at an energy state that is non-judgmental, and operating from a state of acceptance, compassion, love, and peace, you will be connecting with the field of Infinite Intelligence, and reflecting the Divine essence of Pure Consciousness at the worldly level. At one with this state of consciousness, the field of Infinite Intelligence will always unfold in your favor.

Whatever we place our attention on expands in our lives. If you focus on the deep, fundamental needs of your Self, you will manifest deep rewards. The deep essential needs of our soul include love, a meaningful life purpose, creativity, a sense of personal fulfillment, and peace. If you focus instead on the superficial needs of your ego, all of which revolve around the material, impermanent physical world, you will manifest superficial and fleeting rewards. Once again, you attract according to your state of consciousness, and the Universe's mirror reflects what you are, what you think, what you believe, and expands in your life whatever you focus your attention on.

When something belongs to you under the Right of Consciousness, it implies that, when something has apparently been "taken" or deviated from your path, if it rightfully belongs to you, you will receive it, even if by different means or through another vehicle or medium. When I say that something "belongs" or "rightfully corresponds" to you, I do not mean it in terms of possession. We have already delved into the topic that, on the level of a Consciousness of Wholeness, beyond a reality of fragmentation, nothing in the material world belongs to us. We simply have a "turn" to enjoy the benefits that Cosmic Intelligence (God) bestows on us, understanding full well that this world and its contents are impermanent and its pleasures are ephemeral. When I say that something belongs to you under the Right of Consciousness, I am referring to the fact that the Universe has a balanced accountability system and no debt ever goes unpaid in terms of Karma or the natural flow of the Universe (Divine Justice). So, if at any moment you observe that the unconscious acts of the co-participants in your life detour a benefit that was coming your way (you were robbed, defrauded, you were over-looked for a new position at work, etc.), the unconscious acts contributing to those effects will have their consequences, and you will never lose your reward. Of course, this is true as long as you remain aligned to your authentic self, in a state of consciousness of high frequency without violating any of the universal principles where Universal Love operates.

When you align with the state of Pure Consciousness, you trust that you create from the source of your True Self, your infinite and creative fountain spring. You trust in your authentic power and, centered in your essence, you recognize that you are complete and are therefore not missing anything. Within this higher state, you have access to Divine wisdom and can attract and manifest all your desires while aligned with Universal Intelligence. When you align with your True Self, your external life reflects your internal state of wholeness, you become grounded in the consciousness of abundance of the Higher Self, of authentic power rather than with the false power of the ego. From this state of consciousness, you are no longer fooled by the insignificant crumbs that the ego ambitiously craves, desires which are grounded in a consciousness of scarcity (unconsciousness) where the ego insatiably grasps at whatever it innocently believes lacking in itself.

When you detach from results and instead become one with the infinite field which is the source of your origin, you live in the truth. You trust in the truth, that you are at once the source and the fulfillment of your goal in one, because your intention, your desire, and the fulfillment of your goals abide within you. We return to the universal principle that the end and the means are one and the same, they are One-Self.

THE IMPORTANCE OF GRATITUDE

The foundation of joy and abundance is our gratitude for all the beautiful things that manifest themselves in our lives. In the U.S., we celebrate Thanksgiving Day each November. The first colonizers of our nation celebrated the first Thanksgiving marking the gratitude, generosity, and bonds of friendship with Native Americans for an abundant harvest after having suffered great hardship and misfortune during their first harsh winter in Massachusetts. Aside from its historical significance, I love the intention of Thanksgiving Day: a time for reflection, a celebration of abundance and appreciation for life's gifts and for the people with whom we share them. With the grace of our gratitude, these gifts of precious moments continue to multiply themselves daily for each and every one of us.

We already know the principal of attraction, that whatsoever we choose to focus our attention on, grows and expands in our lives. Gratitude is a nutriment that activates the energy of attraction in our lives. The more grateful we are, the more we align with abundance consciousness and with the field of Infinite Universal Intelligence. The more whole, integrated and firmly planted you are in the fertile terrain of your Being, acting with mindful presence and conscious intentions at every moment, the more you align with the natural rhythm of the Universe which in turn unfolds, activating with it the energy of attraction effortlessly.

The more you practice gratitude, the more you will see that this positive approach also results in emotional and physical healing effects that place into circulation a series of biochemical reactions that activate your internal pharmacy. Gratitude connects you with the peaceful wisdom of nature where you receive the support of the Universe, becoming the means by which it expresses itself and reflects through you the same abundance, generosity, and perfection of the Universe in your life and the world around you.

Gratitude is a state of consciousness where nothing is taken for granted. It is a recognition of the countless gifts bestowed on us daily without us having to ask: the sun's warm rays, a starlit night, the nourishing rain, the miracle of each breath, the gift of a smile, to name a few. Each day I am humbly grateful for the abundance and generosity of Life itself for these are the "little that maketh up the greatest happiness" indeed, as <u>Friedrich Nietzsche</u> once wrote.[10] These are the most meaningful and invaluable gifts, those which frequently go unnoticed in light of their sheer simplicity, those gifts that money cannot buy.

Why do these moments awaken such happiness? Because these small, simple moments occupy such little space within you that they catalyze your awakening, activating the inherent state of your spirit in a way that envelops you in sublime joy the source of which is your True Self—they drive your direct connection to the state of Pure Consciousness. These small moments in themselves do not produce your happiness but instead, make you aware of your Pure Consciousness and the expansive state of your internal refuge. When you become conscious of this opening in your soul, the inner space of silence and stillness becomes clearly unveiled to you, the space where your True Self and True state of unconditional Happiness reside. This space has always dwelled within you, your expanded consciousness has always been a part of you, but like a dark veil, the conditioning of old patterns hid the light of your Being and your inherent state of Happiness from your sight.

This state of Happiness is a state of consciousness, not an emotion. Emotions are ephemeral, impermanent. The superficial happiness of the physical world is a fleeting emotion, like a feather blown by the wind, it escapes from your fingers no matter how much you try to hold on to it. True Happiness is a deep state with a solid foundation, an inherent state of your Higher Self. The more connected you are to your Higher State of Being, at one with the frequency of understanding, non-judgment, compassion, love and peace, the more integrated you become to the state of True Happiness. To dwell in this state does not mean that you will never feel sadness at some point in your life. It also does not mean that you should downgrade life's many pleasures or that you should be exempt from their full enjoyment. What it means is that you recognize the difference between sadness and joy in terms of transient emotions pertaining to a fragmented reality and the duality of the physical world. You recognize that these unpleasant feelings too will pass, yet your state of True Happiness, which abides within you, prevails as the unequivocal background state of your soul which sustains you. It reflects from within you as the expansive inner peace and wisdom of the field of Oneness which extends beyond the physical world—a state in which the consciousness of your Being is One with the infinite consciousness of the Universe.

It is important to recognize that True Happiness is unconditional. The moment you impose conditions on your happiness you are, in fact, creating limitations and the terms of your suffering and dissatisfaction with life. For example, this means that if as a condition for happiness you envision, the house of your dreams, the perfect body, the perfect bank account balance, or the perfect man or woman that fulfills the countless list of requirements for your happiness, when these conditions fail, you alone are responsible for having framed your own state of unhappiness, dissatisfaction, and suffering. We are all born with the key to happiness, love and peace as these dwell within us. You need only rediscover the truth that you have long forgotten.

True Happiness is a state of consciousness, not an emotion. Happiness is a decision, a conscious choice to remove limiting conditions for its full expression. This natural state reveals itself when we remove all the superfluous conditions that we impose on the perfect equation that we expect will add up to "happiness." We cannot fool ourselves into this authentic state of consciousness. True Happiness cannot be improvised. Within this state of consciousness you cannot "believe" or "think" you are happy, or believe that happiness is a destination. Grounded in this state of consciousness you are convinced that Happiness is the state of delighting in the inner path itself. You align and fuse with the path until you become one with it, and at that moment you know that you Are Happiness.

So, do not wait for grand moments in life, instead take time to gladden your heart with daily gratitude for the small, precious moments that life bestows on us each day. Nourish your intentions with gratitude. Align your intentions with the depth of your Being where your innate state of Happiness reigns. With the wisdom of these secrets, you will activate the energy of attraction to fulfill all your desires and manifest abundance in your life.

EXERCISE

DAILY GRATITUDE

One of my favorite daily habits is writing down three things for which I am grateful each day in my journal. I occasionally read it, reviewing the previous days, months and years, and I always marvel that the moments which have given me the greatest joy are the smallest of occasions shared with my loved ones and enjoying nature. When I review these winks in time, I relive them with relish, smiling with my lips and with my soul, thankful once more for having lived those moments which continue to cultivate my spirit with a continuous state of joy and gratitude for life's generosity. All challenging circumstances suddenly blur before these moments of pure joy and abundance. My heart expands with spiritual happiness that springs from the intimate space that allows me to receive so much love and abundance from life.

I recommend that you integrate into your practice the exercise of writing at least three things for which you are grateful every day. It is a lovely review each night before bedtime that will keep you sensitive to the gifts life offers you daily. It keeps you awakened to the infinite abundance of the Universe and the inherent Happiness of your Being, to which you always have access. I trust that this exercise will bring you as many benefits as it has me and that you will perceive a spiritual opening and immediate transformations in your life with this practice.

10

DETACHMENT AND
UNCERTAINTY

"Detachment is not that you should
own nothing, but that nothing should
own you." ~ Ali Ibn Abi Talib

When you are rooted in the fullness of your true Self,
where your state of consciousness is Happiness, and
where the abundance of the Universe is evident, you
gain an authentic confidence before life as you begin to
see the harmonious display of Divine Intelligence within
each trace of life. Connected to this state of Wholeness,
you recognize your essence, you recognize that the
abundance of the Universe is your birthright and you
recognize that the access key resides in you. Your key
is the cultivation of intentions and actions grounded
in your Self as well as the continuous activation of the
energy of attraction and of your state of Happiness
through the daily nourishment of gratitude. When you
live in this new state of consciousness, you begin to

liberate yourself from attachments and from the fear of uncertainty.

Attachment is the most common cause of suffering. Attachment to things, people, and situations surfaces from the fear of losing what we desire, want, love or "possess" in life. The problem is that we live in the physical world where nothing is permanent. We know this intellectually, but at the personal level, we live in a constant state of denial over the impermanence of the world, of our loved ones and the content of our lives. Quite commonly, suffering results when these escape, disappear or we think of the potential loss of those we love and the things we most desire. However, nothing in this world lasts forever. Nothing in this world belongs to us. Not even our own bodies belong to us. Skin, bones and tendons will someday transform into ashes and dust, blown by the wind through time and space. Once upon a time our atoms shaped the stars and we will once again return to being stardust in the wind, like grains of sand in the infinite ocean of the universe.

Now, the practice of detachment does not imply that you should desire nothing or that you should "not own anything, but that nothing should own you" (Ali Ibn Abi Talib 599-661AD). When you practice detachment, you acknowledge that nothing in this lifetime of impermanence belongs to you and, as such, you are grateful for the opportunity that was bestowed on you to enjoy them, live them deeply and relish in them, including the people you love and who form a part of your life. You are also grateful for the miraculous opportunity of having incarnated into this human experience. From the thousands of reproductive sperm cells and hundreds of egg cells, your unique formation materialized itself to live this experience and perceive it through your eyes, feel it through your flesh and absorb it with your individual consciousness. You might have just as easily not been embodied or experienced this marvelous existence.

Detachment implies a state of acceptance where one lets things flow as they do, without being attached to what we expect or wish them to be, and without forcing solutions or results onto any given situation. However, you must not confuse detachment with resignation or disinterest, instead, it means that you act with your attention and intentions clearly focused on your desires and connected to the authentic power of your Higher Self. It implies your surrender, faith or trust in the Universe and in the Divine Intelligence that moves the entire cosmos. It means that you offer no resistance or opposition to the natural unfolding of the Universe and that you are no longer taking a defensive stance in the face of transitory life situations. Rather than being aligned to the unconscious perceptions of ego, thinking in terms of scarcity and with actions grounded in fear of loss or attachment to what you wish to gain, you instead align with the creative frequency of the abundant universal reservoir where the Universe moves effortlessly to manifest your desires.

Paradoxically, the more you align with your True Self and practice detachment to material things and results, the more you will see the development and effortless realization of your goals and desires. What operates here? What operates is your trust and surrender to the wisdom of uncertainty. The universe functions under an infinite organizing power within what may superficially appear as chaos. We have delved into this previously in terms of our responsibility to connect with the higher energy frequencies of acceptance, non-judgmental understanding, love, compassion, and peace, all of which are elements of Divine Intelligence, which is the source of our Self. We have also delved into what it means to expand from a consciousness of fragmentation to a consciousness of Wholeness or Totality, a consciousness that extends beyond duality and our limited perceptions of the physical world and where order and a natural fluidity to the Universe abounds.

When we take responsibility to maintain a consciousness of Wholeness and mindful contemplation of the present moment, with positive and clear intentions, detached from past conditioning, without anxiety over future results, we can clearly perceive the synchronicity of events and people that present themselves at the precise moment in our path for the advancement of our goals. Once again, this requires faith or trust in the organizing power of the Universe, and in an expansive consciousness beyond ego, it requires maintaining your Self aligned to your authentic power and it requires fearlessness under uncertainty, it means maintaining a state of surrender where you let go of your personal will and instead trust the will of the Universe, Divine Intelligence or God.

At times you will experience that the universe does not always deliver what you consider fitting, but instead, that which you truly need for your growth and evolution. This does not take place in a deterministic manner, as if everything is written or predestined for you, instead it happens as you choose your lessons and pave your own path with each step and choice, consciously and unconsciously, thereby creating your own reality and experience of life. From this state of surrender in the face of uncertainty, you are unafraid, in fact, you remain open, flexible and adaptable before every option and possibility proffered by the Universe. As such, your world expands, and your experience of life becomes richer and more spontaneous, you live in a way that is aligned with the nature of the Universe (Divine Intelligence, Tao, Undifferentiated Consciousness) of which you are a part. You embrace uncertainty without reservations, accepting the secret and mysterious discretion of the Universe, like a dynamic and passionate adventure. You move at the same rhythm of the universal dance.

Individuals who call themselves "lucky" or who believe to have "good luck" are people who, whether consciously or not, take advantage of these fundamental principles of the natural flow of the Universe. "Lucky" people are not attached to any particular result. They accept that things may or may not turn out as they desire because they understand that we live in a world of probabilities, therefore, accepting what comes and goes in their lives and trusting that there is a hidden order or reason which presents them with opportunities for new adventures in life. These individuals are generally open and adaptable to change, have confidence in themselves and trust that things will always turn out well for them. They feel capable of taking advantage of even the least desirable developments, understanding them to be indeterminate cycles in perpetual movement, without beginning or end. Although these individuals may not know it as such, they live surrendered to energy ("luck") that favors them (the evolutionary impulse of the Universe), and as such, they are prepared to take full advantage of the synchronistic opportunities presented to them at any given moment. Although it may be unconsciously, these "lucky" individuals are, in effect, accepting the Divine order of all possibilities, they have faith or trust in this order, they display fearlessness because they trust that everything always has a way of turning out well for them, they exhibit detachment from past episodes because, even when something has escaped them, they are confident that it will return or will otherwise be replaced by a better opportunity. How lucky indeed!

When you operate from this state of consciousness, you are aligned with the highest energy frequencies which reflect the wisdom of the hologram or mirror of the Universe, discussed earlier. You simply sow the seeds rooted in this frequency which will germinate into a fruitful bounty, lovingly nourishing them yet unattached to the season in which these fruits will be harvested. You are completely confident that your harvest will take place at the right time, you trust that your August harvest is well assured. You delight in the process without thinking about the end result because joy is your purpose—your joy is the process itself of whatsoever it is you are developing and creating.

When you are operating at this level of faith and surrender, you become one with the Totality and become aware that the fulfillment of your desires unfolds effortlessly because, connected to the Universal Intelligence of the Totality, you yield the fruits of the field of infinite abundance. You observe that the more you trust this wisdom, the more you see immediate results, which instills even more confidence in the face of uncertainty. The more you surrender, the more you merge with the natural flow of the Universe. You begin to lose your attachment to the material things of this world because, with newfound confidence in your authentic power and in the secrets for the manifestation of your desires, you are aware that your access to this infinite wellspring of abundance and possibilities is unlimited.

At this state, you understand that you are a copy machine, as my father often says. Everything that you create is a product of the energy of your intentions, of your actions and of your connection with the natural rhythm of Universal Intelligence. Each time you place your positive energy into circulation using the secrets of manifestation, you are able to recreate the same energy of the material symbols in your life, even if these are "taken" or if they "disappear," because their origin and their manifestation derive from your Self, aligned to Divine Intelligence. You are a creator. Just like a photocopier which has the capability to reproduce an endless amount of images, you are a reproductive generator of energy and of the material symbols that surround you—the symbols of money, houses, cars, employment positions, etc.—manifested in the physical world through your own energy. When you trust this fact, attachments, worries and fears disappear. In short, you reproduce and attract to your life the symbols that are compatible with your own state of consciousness.

Paradoxically, connected to this state of consciousness, you attract more with less effort. Usually, it is at one with this energy state that we begin to cultivate intentions of deeper desires and fulfillments, with an expanded purpose that extends beyond our own personal gratification as the end. It is at this stage that we often begin to cultivate our Dharma, or life purpose, and to cultivate Universal Love.

11

UNIVERSAL LOVE

"He who experiences the unity of life
sees his own Self in all beings, and all
beings in his own Self." ~Bhagavad Gita

The principals that orchestrate the natural flow of Universal Intelligence all merge into one principal—Divine Love or Universal Love. But what is Love, really? Love, as described in the physical world we experience, is a fleeting emotion like so many other feelings. Love as an emotion is derived from the same source that gives rise to our limited perceptions of the physical world. Feelings are all impermanent and mutable, which is why love, as an emotion, often burns out, dissipates, or is simply transferred easily to another person. The reason for this is that, what many describe as love is oftentimes physical attraction, sexual passion, possessiveness, attachment, desire and/or dependence. All of these feelings are products of ego or the false "self."

True Love, Divine Love or Universal Love, is not an emotion, but rather, a state of consciousness; it is an innate birthright of our True Self, of our expansive Higher Self. Love as a state of consciousness is permanent and does not end or change. Love at this state is inclusive and unconditional, extending to everything and everyone equally without exclusivity or conditions for its expression. When you operate from this state, aligned to the elevated energy frequency of unconditional love or Divine Love, life flows effortlessly, relationships flourish, life's difficult situations are resolved with ease, and you reach your goals with the synchronistic precision of Divine Intelligence in motion. You begin to experience that people become more open, amenable and cooperative with you. At this state, the Universe and life reflect the same energy intensity of the Love that you radiate and contribute to the Universe. Once again, the Universe echoes back the same harmonious melody (energy) that you confer on it.

When you expand into Love as your state of consciousness, you live from the core of your Higher Self rather than from a false, egocentric self-concept. Aligned with the frequency of Love, you live an expansively awakened human condition, as opposed to a limited human experience or what I denominate an unconscious humanity. When you live in a state of unconscious humanity, you are sleepwalking through life, where life's illusory dream state is your only reality. It is a state of existence where ego identity (the false self) dominates our actions and our relationships. It is a state of spiritual myopia where you live life connected or plugged into the collective unconsciousness of your world, your social circle, your nation, etc. Whereas, to live from a state of conscious humanity is to live a human existence that is awakened to an expansive reality that includes both the physical world, as experienced by our senses, as well as the spiritual reality that extends beyond the physical.

Wherever Universal Love resides and is expressed, there is absolutely no room to ever harbor fear, doubt, or negative thoughts and emotions. The power of Love gives us wings to fly as it is the foundation of clear intentions rooted in our hearts and in the authenticity of our Higher Self, where our motivations and purpose are pure, generous, inclusive, unconditional, compassionate and cooperative. It is a holistic state that becomes integrated into each aspect of our lives at the personal and professional levels as well as in our collective participation in our communities. Individuals who are aligned with the energy of Universal Love are characterized by a sense of gratitude before life, by non-judgmental acceptance, humility, and the warmth of loving kindness. Where there is hopelessness and apathy they choose to elevate, unconditionally through Love, whoever needs relief from suffering, as exemplified by Mother Theresa whose life was an example of selflessness, giving, and unconditional love for the most abject and marginalized groups of society.

Living from the state of consciousness of Divine Love, one is able to fully experience the abundant life-giving energy which, just like the sun, provides light, warmth, and nourishment to each of us equally, without distinctions or preferential exclusivities. It is a state of consciousness that originates from the rich, unconditional wellspring of the Universe's Divine Intelligence, a wellspring that gives without judgment, without attachment or any expectations in return, yet it creates, receives and emits its brilliance from the nucleus of its own Divine energy, recharging and nourishing itself from the same sublime and peaceful energy it circulates into the world. At the same time, this infinite wellspring of Universal Love produces fruitful rewards, unconditionally and effortlessly, because its purpose is to Be, to give, to generate and continuously radiate the same replenishing, unquenchable and transcendent energy that originates from its Being.

Love, as a state of consciousness, abides within us like a seed waiting for the opportunity to germinate, flower and make its expression evident in our lives. When we cultivate the energy of Love, it blooms within us, Love infuses all our actions and intentions, it engulfs us and we in turn project it into the world and to whom we interact, the fruits of which are effects that are compatible with the same energy that we have placed into circulation, both on the personal and collective levels. Contrary to living on this higher plane, negative emotions block the light of Love from one's life. As such, the more we liberate ourselves from ego's prison and the dark veil of low-frequency emotions and actions (competition, resentment, vengeance, anger, pride, fear, envy, shame, and insecurity), the more we are able to experience the essence of Love within ourselves, in our surroundings and in the nature of life itself each day.

If we were to face life, our relationships and the situations we face daily from the state of consciousness of Universal Love, we would be availing ourselves of the most powerful survival tool that exists in the Universe. Love is the driving energy that moves the entire cosmos. Love is authentic power, the opposite of ego's false concept of power whose pursuit is to control and obtain results by way of force.

The energy of Love is also an authentic source of healing and transformation. Many authors have written and documented their own experiences of healing as a result of connecting with the energy of Universal Love and the practice of daily gratitude and compassion. The endorphins (hormones which prolong our lives and promote our health) which we secrete from the state of consciousness of Love not only flood us with authentic Happiness but also work to unblock toxic emotions locked in the energetic centers of our bodies which are the frequent cause of illnesses. By unblocking toxic energy, Love restores the natural harmony and balance of our own internal pharmacy thereby bolstering our intrinsic power of spontaneous self-healing.

Our loved ones, our pets and oftentimes nature's simple beauty, all serve to catalyze our inherent state of Love. In this deep state of authentic Love, we are capable of loving even the most "villainous" among us when we realize that their actions originate from a limited state where they are unaware of their Being's true essence; they are unaware of the brilliance of their spirit and the Totality that unites us all as One. When we attain this level of deep insight, we realize that even the most heinous of crimes have two victims: that who perpetrates the criminal act as well as the object of the transgression. At this state of awareness, we understand that even the vilest perpetrators are victims of the darkness of their egos, of the past conditioning of their environment, and of low-frequency energy that propels them to act against their fellow man which is the same as acting against themselves. Once you attain the elevated state of consciousness of Universal Love, you feel compassion for these individuals and perceive them, not as evil, but instead as innocent souls who are ignorant of the universal principles. This deeper understanding allows us to see that these individuals live a fragmented reality and that their consciousness is blocked by negative patterns in their lives and by their false sense of "self" which has unfortunately obscured the miracle of true Love in their own souls and blurred Love's reflection in their lives and environment. In short, we gain a new degree of compassion for them, aware that they are in fact victims of an extreme level of unconsciousness and suffering caused by the intense darkness that engulfs them. We now know that they are lost souls in need of Love and Light.

At the level of Universal Love, or Unconditional Love, we see and understand from our True Self, from a state of Wholeness or Totality that unites all sentient beings in this world as One. Once you become interpenetrated in the state of True Love, the Universe's architecture reveals itself to you in each of life's minutia, not as a series of objects and distinctive, independent, living beings but as figures that together compose an intricate, sacred geometry where the forms all slowly integrate amongst themselves until individual forms are no longer distinguishable, and the more you expand your frame of vision, you see that they lose their individual characteristics and interpenetrate into a massive undifferentiated network of light and energy. At this state, you understand that each detail in this network is a product of Divine Love, which is the vital energy and the creative foundation of the Universe, the Divine origin of everything. When you attain this level of consciousness, you live the wholeness and integrity of life and can see your Self clearly reflected in everything. Love ceases to be a personalized or exclusive emotion. Love transforms into a deep state of consciousness that is inclusive or universal, a state in which there is no "you" or "me," "them" or "us," it is a state in which we recognize our Infinite Wholeness, we rediscover the state of our Atemporal Oneness.

LOVE IN ACTION

One day, my father shared with me a beautiful episode that he witnessed. On his return to the office from running errands, he observed a homeless man in the area. The man was very unkempt, and it was evident that he had not eaten in quite some time. He appeared weak, and he lay down on the sidewalk as if he had surrendered all hope and completely given up on life. Suddenly, a young man walks towards him with a pizza box. He sees the homeless man lying on the sidewalk and approaches him, crouches down next to him and hands him a slice of pizza. Surprised, the homeless man stares at the young man with disbelief as he sits alongside him on the sidewalk to join him for lunch. This was an act of true Love. The young man did not care that the homeless man was unkempt or unbathed, he was neither repelled nor afraid of him. The young man saw him with the eyes of his soul, aware of the deep connection and oneness we all share with one another, meeting him from the space of sacred wisdom of Being. It was an act of kindness, compassion, and Love. When you live at this frequency, you transmit your loving energy with the simple act of Being Love in motion. You contribute to an avalanche of Love and compassion through each interaction which echoes back to you the same energy that you radiate into your environment—you receive it without either expecting or asking for it in return. You reap what you are, which in turn keeps the same Happiness and Love that you exude circulating in your life.

DHARMA: THE INTERNAL GPS

We all have an internal GPS which is tuned-in to Divine Intelligence (Universal Consciousness or God) but we may also exercise personal control of the steering wheel and preserve the option of either paying attention, or not, to the GPS (Free Will). If we choose to steer off course, the GPS will recalculate our position providing us with an alternate route to the same destination. The truth of the matter is that regardless of how long it takes us, sooner or later we will get there. Equally so, at the spiritual level life's journey is more easeful when we follow the internal guidance of our True Self. Let us say, using our GPS metaphor that, from the level of our Higher Self, our journey through life is effortless when we are tuned-in to or aligned with our spirit (Infinite Consciousness). Karma is evolution by means of decisions guided by our ego where our mind and false sense of self dominates and where our concept of reality is relative. This is equivalent to controlling the steering wheel through our will rather than by following the GPS's instructions. On the other hand, Dharma is evolution guided by our Higher Self where our awakened consciousness dominates aligned to Universal Intelligence (God, Tao) and where our perception of reality is absolute. We touch a deeper reality—the field of Pure Consciousness, Totality, Wholeness Consciousness, Undifferentiated Consciousness or the Field of Oneness.

UNIVERSAL LOVE AND DHARMA

Once you see your connection with others and begin to navigate the ocean of Universal Love, it is common for you to start asking yourself more frequently, what is my purpose in life (Dharma)? What do I enjoy spending my time doing? You might also ask yourself, How can I serve others?, instead of, how do I take advantage of this person or situation now or in the future? Here you enter the field of your Dharma or life purpose. When you are in Dharma, your life flows effortlessly attracting that which you are to your life, and your decisions throughout your life journey are centered on remaining authentic to your true essence or Higher Self. At this level of Being, you accelerate your spiritual evolution by vibrating at an energy of higher frequency that is characterized by acceptance, kindness, compassion, Universal Love and peace.

When you are living your Dharma, your primary purpose is to manifest the field of Oneness (what we are) into this physical world in which we live. You align yourself with your True Self, cultivating your spiritual path, aligning your intentions and actions for your chosen external purpose in the physical world with your inner, spiritual purpose, which is to manifest Love, compassion, and peace. Awakened to this state of consciousness, to live and to act in terms of the natural spiritual flow of Divine Intelligence becomes your primary purpose or Dharma, manifesting fruitful rewards effortlessly at both the personal and collective levels. At this level of existence, everything flows gracefully in rhythm and harmony with the Universe.

From this higher state of consciousness, desiring exclusively for your benefit and the well-being of those closest to you begins to wane. Aware that you are part of a greater Totality, you soon realize that by safeguarding the welfare of all sentient beings, which you no longer perceive as separate from yourself, you are concurrently protecting your own progress and contentment, recognizing that you equally benefit as part of that Totality. Your insight originates from a state of consciousness of Oneness where there is no separation between you and the rest of the world. You realize that what benefits and protects others, the world, and the earth, also helps and protects you.

Unfortunately, some may believe that the gain of others implies their personal loss, but this type of thinking comes from the unconsciousness of ego. In reality, there is no loss or gain in the Universe where there is a perfect balance and accountability system. In fact, when you fully immerse yourself in the frequency of Universal Love, you realize that the happiness and abundance of others do not diminish you in any way. Instead, they contribute to your own state of happiness and wealth. As the Buddha so eloquently expressed, "Thousands of candles can be lighted from a single candle, and the life of the candle will not be shortened. Happiness never decreases by being shared."

The Universe is an unlimited reservoir of abundance which is awaiting for you to submerge completely within it with absolute trust and full abandon, so that you may fully benefit from its unquenchable resources of which there are more than enough for everyone to partake. Living from this state of consciousness, we are able to experience spiritual wholeness within our very own unique human embodiment and existence. If we were to collectively unite in this state of Universal Love consciousness and higher purpose, we would advance great strides not just individually but as a nation and as a global community. It would require thinking, acting, and living with a consciousness grounded in Oneness, inclusion, and Universal Love. Aligned to this state where

Love and purpose converge, our Dharma or external purpose reflects the expansive spiritual consciousness of our Higher Self or Inner Master.

When we do what we love, we connect with our inner state of Happiness. When we are deeply connected to our Higher Self (Pure Consciousness, Undifferentiated, Consciousness, the Tao or God) our personal fulfillment is naturally obtained from cultivating our talents and doing what we love as a positive contribution to the lives of others—we become of service to others through our love and inner bliss. When we are of service to others, we ask ourselves, "How may I be of assistance," instead of "What can I gain from this interaction?; we are a part of the solution in every situation we encounter, from a perspective of compassion for our shared humanity and oneness of spirit at the level of our soul or awakened Higher Self.

When you are fulfilling your Dharma, or purpose, Being becomes more important than doing. This means that aligning with your Higher Self (Undifferentiated Consciousness, the Tao, Dharmakaya, Allah, God, or Pure Consciousness) becomes your primary purpose and your Being imbues everything that you execute. For example, if you are an artist, a poet, a musician or an individual who is aligned to your Higher Self, you and what you do merge into one. The artist is art, the poet is poetry, the musician is music, and the individual on the path of light is generosity, love, peace, and compassion. The artist, for example, creates because of her innate passion and from a sincere and sacred place, propelled by her inevitable need to transmit her soul in an atemporal union with the receptor. At this level of interpenetration between your Self and your purpose, or Dharma, you have no other choice but to give birth to the deepest part of your Being through everything you chose to undertake and develop, even the simplest of activities. Your every action is stamped with the authentic seal of your Higher Self.

This is the process that many describe as creating by means of inspiration. The etymology of the word inspiration originates from the Latin *inspirare* which means inhalation, to introduce air into the body or lungs, but it also means divine enlightenment prior to creation. This state of inspiration comes from a direct connection to Divine Intelligence or Pure Consciousness. Creating and acting on the basis of this state means the act of breathing Infinite Intelligence from the centered stillness and wisdom of your Self and exhaling your gift to the physical world of forms. When you are focused, performing whatever reveals the inherent state of Happiness and Love of your inner Being, you enter an atemporal zone where time dissipates and whatsoever you create is eternity in motion materializing in the world of forms.

If you are a musician, your instrument is a continuity of your own Self—the musician and the instrument converge into one unified piece. Centered in the stillness and silence of your Higher Self, you Are Oneness and tranquility, and the harmony and beauty of Divinity itself flows through you like a thread that unites your soul with the infinite soul of the Universe. Everything that originates from this sacred space of your spirit, from the depth of your authentic Self, is a Divine expression. At this level of authentic expression, aligned with your Dharma, Being is more important than doing or receiving, but paradoxically, you attract that which you are and therefore, success and abundance at both the spiritual and material level are never far from reach.

In practical terms, this means that no matter what your trade, profession or station in life (artist, nurse student, police officer, laborer, mother, husband, waiter, cook, attorney, doctor, gardener, politician, CEO of a company or president of a nation, etc.) when you converge the most intimate and sacred Light of your authentic Self with your intentions and actions throughout your own journey and movement in life, the result is an abundant display of Love, happiness, and authenticity, both in your personal interrelations as well as in everything you undertake, placing into circulation and attracting the same gifts you offer others into your own life and environment.

The secret is to remain aligned to the authentic power of your Inner Master (Higher Self), to dedicate your time and energy working at whatever you happen to love and enjoy while offering the same things you love, desire, and enjoy to others, always rooted in Oneness and Universal Love. In this way, you will unlock the opening to the true expression of Happiness, Love, and Peace that reside within you, attracting more of that which you radiate out into the world. The Happiness of others becomes your own Happiness, your Love of others permeates you with Love, and the Peace of your immediate surroundings and the world flood you with Peace.

12

FLOWERING SEASON

"Open your eyes and come—
Return to the root of the root
of your own soul…" ~ Rumi

The Tree of Life is a universal design prevalent in various religious traditions, as well as in biology, philosophy, and mythology. This image appears in different cultural traditions initiating from Pre-Columbian times in Mesoamerica and the continents of China and Europe. Numerous writings and diverse reproductions of the iconic image can be found in the traditions of Buddhism, Christianity, Hinduism, Islam and Kabbalah.

There are countless versions of the Tree of Life, but my favorite is the one depicting a tree with lush, exuberant foliage and deep, solid roots usually framed in a circle. The image represents the perfect symmetry existing between that which lies beneath the earth and that which is manifested outside it. As it is above, so it is below. Turning the image upside down, you see a reflection of the same attributes. The roots reflect the fruits and the fruits reflect the roots. The circle symbolizes the circle of life, the connection with all of creation and the Oneness or Totality of the Universe.

First, we must know in which terrain we are rooted. Are you rooted in the fertile, expansive, abundant terrain of your True Self, Divine Intelligence, Pure Consciousness (God) or in ego's small vase which is the limited, arid ground of human unconsciousness and the false sense of self? No matter how grand, ornate, and majestic the vessel where you intend to plant your seeds appears, it is but a limited space; it will never provide the proper space or conditions to nourish your roots for your maximum healthy growth and deep fulfillment. The roots will seek to escape from the vase to find nourishment and expansion. The roots of that which hopes to germinate will lack the room to grow and bear fruits because of the vase's restricted space. You need to sow seeds in the ample fertile terrain of the Totality, the fertile ground of your spiritual essence (Pure Consciousness) where the abundance of the Universe unfolds in the blooming field of your heaven on earth, the Eden of your creation which you cultivate with the wisdom of your spiritual gardening. Destroying the vessel (ego), you find freedom to grow and develop to the full expression of your True Self which is an inherent need. Your fruits and colorful blooms will nourish you and others attracting the same joy and vividness to life that you enflame in others and that you contribute to your environment.

The steps are:

1. Recognize who you are. Return to the root of your Being (Infinite Consciousness or Divine Intelligence), the reflection of Universal Intelligence

on earth, which is the part in you that contains everything in the universal hologram.

2. Become rooted in your True Self. This means to re-establish your connection to your Higher Self (True Self) with your expanded consciousness in a state that extends beyond your ego.

3. Transform your perceptions, intentions, and thoughts. Here you cultivate and internally strengthen the connection to your roots keeping them rooted firmly in the awakened state of consciousness of your Higher Self.

4. Always act within our physical world by externalizing and creating on the foundation of who you are, Pure Consciousness, the Divine Intelligence of your true spiritual essence.

If you align yourself with your ego—the physical world and a false perception of yourself—you will be cultivating roots in a false foundation and your perceptions, intentions, thoughts, and actions will be grounded in unconsciousness, in the world of impermanence, of fleeting pleasures and suffering.

Your roots penetrate much deeper than the material world we live in; they run deeper and beyond your family heritage, your race, your nationality, and your culture. Your roots delve deeply into the field of Infinite abundance, creativity and the field of all possibilities. The actual roots of your soul are of Divine origin; they derive from the field of Totality where we all merge into one. So, just as Rumi summons us, open your eyes and return to the root of the root of your own soul. Within that space you desire nothing, yet, you hold everything. There you will find ultimate delight in your long sought after treasure.

We can recognize the depth of our roots when we penetrate in the sacred space of our Self, of our spirit. Here we discover that, in spite of the harshest and darkest of winters, all things rooted and nourished are waiting to blossom to the fullest expressions of their souls. To blossom, to grow, and to create are natural and innate desires, the evolutionary impulse of the spirit and the human condition. Always remain faithful to this instinct. Rooted in the heart of Being, you initiate your path towards wisdom and freedom where you awaken to the flowering garden of our own inner Spring.

There is no one path. As the Buddha once expressed in a parable, words and teachings serve as guides, and these guides are like rafts used to cross to the opposite shore of the river. After crossing and reaching solid ground, you let the raft go. The Buddha concluded, "So it is with my teachings, which are like a raft, and are for crossing over with — not for seizing hold of." The path is one in the sense that it directs us all to the same inner space, just like the needles of a compass pointing us in the direction of True North. The path is the return path to ourselves, the return home; it is the return to your Higher Self, your spirit, your Awakened Consciousness, and your Hidden Paradise. Everyone sets out on their own path. You level out your own road with each stride. You are a landscape artist designing the way to the hidden paradise of your inner garden. Each path is personalized. You personalize your pathway with your steps, your perceptions, your intentions, your thoughts, your experiences and with your state of consciousness. It is in this sense that each spiritual path is different, but no path is better than any other. You cannot and should not compare them. Each one initiates the path of their own inner journey at their own pace. It is not at all important how fast or slow your strides are, only that you embark on the voyage, that you cultivate the path and remain steadfast on your journey. Each person's internal spiritual path is an intimate one, and each path is perfect.

Just as one cannot force fruit trees to ripen out of season, our awareness too can only flower in the spring of its own timely awakening. So, dedicate your energy to cultivating and tending your garden with tenderness and infinite patience and lovingly water and nourish the seeds of Love and Compassion, of Happiness and inclusiveness, so that these may grow and develop deep, strong roots. Your fruits will ripen in the perfect season offering real nourishment, and your blooms will bring unparalleled joy to yourself and others, a nourishment and joy that will span all seasons.

Then one day, amidst your blooming grove, you will awaken to the illuminating wisdom that the right season for this flowering does, after all, always take place in the season of NOW, a season that can never arrive either too early or too late, and in that wondrous revelation, you will smile with the same gratitude and bliss of the great sages.

EPILOGUE

COMPLETING THE CIRCLE

Our deepest desire is to feel whole or complete. My inner journey was propelled by that same innate desire. Throughout my journey, I have been able to discover that genuine Happiness and True Love are states of consciousness rather than emotions as I once believed. I have also learned that the smallest of Life's pleasures serve to awaken our inherent state of Love and Happiness. They help to awaken the simple state of pure consciousness which is our genuine Self and is quite often masked by our ego until that crucial moment when we decide to turn our focus towards the wisdom of our inner space. Our Self awaits nonjudgmentally, with infinite patience and compassion for the moment of our sweet homecoming.

I have learned that by discovering who we are not, we arrive at who we truly are and recognize our purpose or direction in life—we free ourselves from the prison of our past burdens, from the negative emotions of the ego, and we find the true meaning of genuine Happiness and Love because, as long as our consciousness remains asleep, we seek happiness and love were they can never be found, in material things and ephemeral feelings, creating attachments to the illusions of life.

Every day I avow my inner knowingness that I am consistently more whole and therefore more fully myself the deeper I submerge myself in the intimate space of my Being. Every day and every interaction offer me new and unexpected experiences to learn and gain greater insight, new territories to discover and endless opportunities to penetrate even deeper on the path to higher consciousness. I can see more clearly the synchronicity of events, the intelligence of the Universe and the natural flow of life, of which I am immensely grateful. I find that silence and stillness, as well as mindful breathing, meditation, and nature, permeate me with a deep, inner peace where I experience simply that I AM, at the purest most authentic state of Being. It is where I find the root of my Self, free of all labels, free of all chains to my past and future, awake in the here-now of the present moment.

Charting out my inner voyage has helped me find a right balance, both personally and professionally, allowing me to converge my inner purpose (remaining on my spiritual path aligned to my Self) with my external purpose (everything else that I accomplish in the physical world). I have been able to reach a level of acceptance and compassion for the multi-layered veil of my "false self," which at one time enshrouded my vision, and compassion for the "false selves" of the broken souls that composed a part of my personal and ancestral past. I have been slowly surrendering unproductive emotions associated with my personal decisions and the actions of others all of which have unfolded in my continuous state of awakening, beyond a litany of lamentations where I now understand that each one (of them and I) have done the best we could, each of us from our own sense of self and from our respective states of consciousness at any given point in time. On the day-break of this new stage in my life, I see without looking and with greater clarity—I see with the eyes of Being. I consider myself a traveler on a journey without a final destination where I continue learning, growing, and cultivating my path daily. My inner journey is my primary purpose and in this purpose I feel the greatest joy.

You too have access to this sublime state of wholeness and inner peace beyond suffering. The physical world of forms delivers the lessons we need for our daily spiritual practice; we do not need to go very far. This inner spiritual journey is the path to rediscovering your Self, to reconnecting with the truth that you have long since forgotten yet have always known intuitively from the subtle murmur issuing from the spring of your soul. The deeper you penetrate on your path, the richer your revelations with each stratum you excavate. Delving deep, you will discover the truth of who you are. You will recognize that your soul is the soul of the universe that becomes conscious of itself through you, thereby completing the circle of an intimate and infinite relationship where you finally decipher the mystery of your origin and recognize that you are the state of Wholeness or Oneness. You trust in the wisdom of uncertainty embracing it fearlessly, with open arms, like a miraculous opening conducive to creativity, expansion, and spiritual evolution which will also reflect material rewards. Here you have complete trust in the order and perfect synchrony of the Universe which unfolds at your feet. You discover that your desires and the desires of the Universe are one and the same. You discover that the Universe whispers its desires through silence and stillness where your spirit resides, where you hear with your soul, and you surrender as the perfect channel to manifest the will of the Universe in the physical world of forms. It is a state of grace and surrender, of faith or trust, where you are interpenetrated with the Universe, and everything flows effortlessly. Here, in this state, even if you are alone you do not feel empty or lonely.

No one can explain this state precisely because it extends beyond the limitations of the intellect, of concepts and words. This experience is a personal one shared with Divinity, an experience that unites us all, a state in which you know that you Are Peace, Are Happiness, Are Love. You no longer see yourself as a fragmented individual in a fragmented world. You no longer view yourself as an incomplete person with missing or broken pieces. What you once perceived as the incoherent pieces of the jigsaw puzzle of your life are now seen to converge in the elements that compose the colorful texture of the rich, elaborate patterns of a gorgeous tapestry that you continue to weave with your intentions and actions. You are One with the Divine Consciousness of the Universe. You touch the deep reality of what you Are with that which you Are—your Pure Consciousness—and your heart beats in unison with the heart of the Infinite Universe. Your inner journey is like an infinite circle in perpetual movement, without beginning or end, one that you begin and continue cultivating and nourishing from the expansive depth of your Integral Self.

I wish you a blissful journey on the way to your own inward blooming garden. We shall meet along the way!

REFERENCES

Banks, C. (1995) *The Essential Rumi*. San Francisco: Harper Collins

Bell's Theorem. (2015, May 26). In *Wikipedia, The Free Encyclopedia*. Retrieved 23:36, August 9, 2015 from https://en.wikipedia.org/w/index.php?title=Bell%27s_theorem&oldid=759017451

Capra, F. (1975, 1999) *The Tao of Physics*, 4th ed. Massachusetts: Shambala Publications, Inc.

Chopra, D. (1994) *The Seven Spiritual Laws of Success*. California: Amber-Allen Publishing

Chopra, D. (2004) *The Book of Secrets*. New York: Three Rivers Press

Dyer, W. (2014) *I Can See Clearly Now*. EEUU: Hay House, Inc.

Hanh, T. (1990) *Our Appointment with Life: Sutra on Knowing the Better Way to Live Alone*. U.S.A.: Parallax Press

Hanh, T. (1998, 2013) *The Heart of the Buddha's Teachings*. U.S.A.: Harmony Books

Hawkins, D. (2004) *Power VS. Force: The Hidden Determinants of Human Behavior*. U.S.A.: Hay House, Inc.

Hawkins, D. (2012) *Letting Go: The Pathway to Surrender*. U.S.A.: Hay House, Inc.

Joel Silver (Producer) & The Wachowski Brothers (Directors). (1999). *The Matrix* (Film). U.S.A.: Warner Bros.

Tolle, E. (2005) *A New Earth: Awakening to Your Life's Potential*. New York: Dutton, Penguin Group.

Zukav, G. (1989, 2014) *The Seat of the Soul: 25th Anniversary Edition*. New York: Simon & Schuster.

NOTES

1   Capra, F. (1975, 1999) The Tao of Physics, 4th ed. Massachusetts: Shambala Publications, Inc. (pp. 310-313)

2   Kinesiology is a technique used to measure a participant's muscle strength while presented with varying stimuli. The studies of David Hawkins, M.D., reveal that negative and false stimuli weaken our muscular strength while positive stimuli and those founded on truth strengthen our muscular power. Hawkins, D. (1995) Hay House, Inc., Power vs. Force: The Hidden Determinants of Human Behavior

3   The logarithmic measurement represents a progressive value. For example, the level 300 does not represent two times 150 but rather 10 to the power of 300 (10^{300}). What this means is that an increment of only a few points significantly increases an individual's power level (energy level) and results in an enormous advancement in an individual's state of consciousness.

4   Hawkins, D. (2012) Hay House, Inc., Letting Go: The Pathway of Surrender, pp 194-196

5   Ibid

6   Ibid

7   Hawkins, D. (1995) Hay House, Inc., Power vs. Force: The Hidden Determinants of Human Behavior, pp 93-94, 261, 273, 275

8   Hanh, T. (2010) Parallax Press, Our Appointment with Life, Sutra on Knowing the Better Way to Live Alone, p.9-11

9   Van Gogh, Vincent (1889) Starry Night, Museum of Modern Art, (MOMA) New York

10 Nietzsche, Friedriche, Thus Spake Zarathustra: A Book for All and None (New York: Viking, 1954), p. 288

Printed in the United States
By Bookmasters